Resilie

Stories of Adult Learning

A learner voice co-production

Edited by Tara Furlong and Keiko Yasukawa

Copyright and Publishing

First published in the United Kingdom in 2016 by RaPAL, Sysondale, Anslow Lane, Rolleston on Dove, DE13 9DS

Available online at http://rapal.org.uk/resilience

A CIP catalogue record of this book is available from the British Library

ISBN 978-0-9513407-1-4 (unabridged e-book .epub)

ISBN 978-0-9513407-2-1 (unabridged Kindle e-book .mobi)

ISBN 978-0-9513407-3-8 (unabridged pdf)

ISBN 978-0-9513407-4-5 (unabridged paperback)

Abridged editions published simultaneously in Australia in 2016 by ACAL, PO Box 2283, Canberra ACT 2601 http://acal.edu.au/

ISBN 978-0- 9953723-2-0 (abridged e-book .epub)

ISBN 978-0- 9953723-1-3 (abridged Kindle e-book .mobi)

ISBN 978-0- 9953723-0-6 (abridged pdf)

ISBN 978-0- 9953723-3-7 (abridged paperback)

No stories in this publication should be taken as an endorsement of any given form of educational provision for any given learner.

Foreword

THIS IS A collection of learner stories, in their own words and with some helpful contributions by tutors along the way. It is testimony to the resilience of human lives, the critical role of lifelong learning, and how adult literacies weave through our journeys, visibly and invisibly. The editors thank each of the learners and their tutors for contributing, Festival of Learning for supporting, and RaPAL (Research and Practice in Adult Literacies) and ACAL (Australian Council for Adult Literacy) for publication.

Lottie Napangardi Robertson

What is resilience? It is our capacity to deal with difficult situations.

Twenty years ago, my husband, my family and I travelled to Lajamanu. Before coming to the Granites, our car broke down. It had a radiator problem. So, we didn't have much water and we started to get upset because we had little ones with us. Our water supply started to get low and also the food was all eaten, so we didn't know what to do. We didn't want to spend another day, so we decided to make a big bush fire so that the people from the Granites could see the smoke and so that someone will come and help us get back home. An hour later someone finally came and brought us back to Yuendumu. So, next time I take my grandchildren, I must make sure we have a vehicle that is in good condition and always let families know ahead when we leave the community.

Contents

Introduction

LEARNER STORIES WERE collected from across Australia and the United Kingdom, and include voices spanning much of the earth. The anthology originated in two national adult literacies organisations whose members wanted told the stories of the resilience of learners and the value of developing literacies through lifelong and lifewide learning. This is the latest collection in a tradition of learner narratives and publications. The contributors were keen to inspire and reassure peers into participation, and to thank the tutors and institutions who helped change their lives, who travelled and supported them during their learning journeys.

IN PRESENTING THEIR writing, many learners realised increasing confidence, supporting children and grandchildren, and opportunities in current and future voluntary roles and employment. Learners experienced the therapeutic benefit of social, creative and learning activity, as many worked through trauma and tragedy, through every form of loss, ill health, difficulty, disability, addiction, abuse, disruption, instability and struggles through state interventions, to learning in the later stages in life. Each story has been tagged and indexed with themes, which makes them searchable as well as browsable in the e-book, paperback and website versions. There is a Glossary of common acronyms. The website includes a small range of multi-media contributions, including transcripts. Most learners appeared to be eagerly bridging the digital divide.

FOR THE DIVERSITY of learning provision which exists, the response to our call is inspirational. In addition to large adult, further, vocational, higher education and charitable provision, we have encountered a phenomenal range of community activity which builds in learning and outreach work. These may be in schools, neighbourhood groups, religious organisations, or outdoor forest school or allotment plots. We have contributions generated in offender learning, secure care, supported housing, retirement care, and special educational needs expertise, which build towards independent living.

EACH STORY WE hope will find readers who identify, and stories that illuminate the challenges and successes of others. As we read the learners' stories, we see unfolding in front of us the rich personal and intergenerational benefits that are afforded through adult learning provision in diverse sites and diverse modes. We hope you enjoy and disseminate our anthology 'Resilience: Stories of Adult Learning'.

Brett Whiting, TAFE East Coast

Worth the Read, 19/4/2012

All my life I have had an illiteracy problem and it was one of the hardest things to overcome in my life. It's like walking down a path and you hit a brick wall that you can't go around or you can't go over. I have done everything that I want to do in my life besides learning to read and write.

For years I was a single parent bringing up two boys. It was hard when it got time to help them with their homework. I always wanted to go back to school or TAFE to help myself but my kids came first until they left the nest. So, I had a little break for a few years. Then I had a talk to my job provider and she told me how to do something about it. I told myself, "What the heck, I will have a go at this."

It was hard at first, getting my mind around the books. I put my head down and went for it. Reading and writing started to get easier for me and before I knew it, I was reading a book. I never thought I would do that but I'm reading now and I'm enjoying this for the first time in my life. I'm finally reading and writing like there is no tomorrow. It has even opened up new doors for me to explore.

It has changed my life for the better and it has been the second best thing that has happened in life. The first has been my boys, and they have been encouraging me as well.

I can now write my teacher this essay and it comes so naturally. All I can say to my angels is thank you from the bottom of my heart, you have given me a new outlook on life and it's great!

A Peak From Behind, 14/12/2015

Since I left the TAFE class, I went on to do more study. I did a Cert 2 in Auto and followed up with Cert 2 in Engineering, passing successfully in both. All this time during the courses I had a column in the local newspaper. I have been a member of a local sporting shooters' club for quite a few years now, and I am involved in the weapons licensing side of things. I'm now in training to be a TA (trainer assessor) for QLD firearms licensing. I get a kick out of helping people do their test because we ask if anyone has difficulties reading or writing. We will always get a couple, so I sit with them to help. I tell them I can understand what they're going through because I was once like that myself.

I understand why my angels do what they do because I enjoy helping people out who I was once like. I hope they can make it as far as I have with their reading and writing because my future is looking bright.

Tutor Perspective: Margaret Khan

This student embodies the essence of resilience in his learning. The stories have been written three and a half years apart. The first was when Brett finished in his TAFE LLN (language, literacy and numeracy) in 2012, and the second has been written this week to show where his learning journey has taken him since then. He continues to attend a community literacy group, seven years after taking the first tentative steps.

Andy Marsh, TAFE East Coast

when I stirted in 2008 my sehlF conflbene was how
and my will to wright Forms and documenst wa no
Good and my socialrelnteraction was not Good b
won it is Good my social reinteraction with peoly
has in pinproved overall improvment with my
reading has in inproved and my overall conflber
has inproved and my wright documenst and
vorms

Text interpretation as read by student:

When I started in 2008 my self confidence was low and my will to write forms and documents was no good. My social interactions with people was not good but now it is good. My social interactions with people has improved and there has been an overall improvement with my reading. My overall confidence has improved and I write documents and forms.

<u>Tutor Perspective: Margaret Khan</u>

I have chosen to send you the unedited version of Andy's story because his learning journey commenced seven years ago with a learning difficulty in evidence (he struggled to write most Dolch words with letters in the correct order). Andy's hand-written text was completely unaided, and even though he still has literacy difficulties, to reach this point has taken him seven years of faithfully attending a weekly literacy community class. He does not miss a week. This shows true resilience.

Rayleigh Burke, TAFE East Coast

Jason Sauer, a young man who has been to "hell and back", recently came to Gympie TAFE to talk to us and to share his life experience with us. Jason wants to become a motivational speaker. We were the first audience to hear his life-changing story.

Like many young guys on the sunshine coast, he was surfing, snow skiing and partying with his mates and by the time he was sixteen he had a problem with substance abuse. He wasted many of his years moving in and out of re-hab.

Following a fight with his girlfriend on Christmas Day 2010 Jason relapsed on heroin. He overdosed on a friend's floor and was comatose for more than fourteen hours causing a lack of oxygen to his extremities. Jason was fighting for his life. The decision was made to amputate his legs above the knee to save his life. Bouts of depression and further addiction followed. At his lowest point he considered giving up on life. Then salvation in the form of a Facebook friend saved him from hell. Jason connected with the friend who was in an adaptive bobsled driving school in Park City, USA.

Today Jason is fitted with state of the arts microprocessor knees and prosthetic legs, as well as skier and bobsledder gear and he is based at the National Ability Centre, USA.

At the end of the talk he told us that he wasn't there to tell us not to take drugs. This message was clear, the most important things he told us was not to hurt those who love you, and to chase your dreams. Jason, during the course of his life, had lost everything but his passion for skiing saved him. We came away from the talk with many things to think about.

Jason delivered his talk in a raw, honest and passionate way. He left no stone unturned and was willing to answer even the most sensitive of questions. He made a great motivational speaker and we wish him well with his Olympic career.

He's definitely someone we won't forget.

Tutor Perspective: Margaret Khan
This is the story of a motivational speaker who addressed our class and whose resilience inspired our learners.

Star Painter, Learning in Wiltshire

Hi, I am Star and I guess the very beginning of my journey I don't quite remember due to my very full life. I first embarked on a course set up by the lovely ladies from the Family Learning Team in Wiltshire, very much needed at the time, called Time 4 U, and have never looked back. They had inspired something in me: not just to go forward but to help other parent carers succeed in a brighter achievable future. Having set a group up, I needed to do something different to all other groups that seemed to be going stale. I do believe without the support of Lucinda and her lovely tutors, I would never have achieved being here writing this. They saw something in me too.

After attending several more courses, I became so positive in achieving greater things. I then entered employment after enrolling on my third course. Sadly my life and health took a turn for the worst, but this did not stop me continuing my learning. I spent a long time also with my parent carers on so much negativity that it has been amazing to put some fantastic positive learning in the mix to filter through and ignite that spark we all have. I feel very proud of my mums, dads and grandparents who share my journey and who are taking my lead and changing their future. Words simply cannot explain how that feels. I have carers who have anxieties, socialising issues to name a few, and they pushed harder than they have before. I am so very proud of all of them.

This is still the beginning of my journey but my path has changed. I always feel sad to complete a course as today we have all completed our SEAL course. It always leaves me thirsty for more and the lovely team here in Wiltshire keep a tight hold of us and have some amazing courses in the new year for us all. Life and learning stops with you, reach out and take it by both horns and give it some welly.

Tutor Perspective: Lucinda Murray

Star, 37, lives in Wiltshire. She is a single mother and has two children. Three years ago in 2012, she started a carers' group aimed at supporting families who have children with special educational needs. The group, which began with five members, now has fifty families and it is growing from strength to strength. Star promotes adult learning; both formal and informal. Her passion and belief in improving lives through learning has developed from an often difficult path.

Star experienced family domestic violence and was a heroin addict. She became estranged from her Cornish family. In 2005 she made the decision to build bridges with her family and to turn her life around. She attended a rehabilitation project and underwent CBT for a year. Her return to Cornwall led her to supporting vulnerable women; prolific offenders who were involved with repeated petty crimes. She trained the groups to be volunteers, supporting their local community. Her vision to support others stayed with her when she became a mum.

Having moved to Wiltshire, Star then found herself in a challenging partnership which has resulted in her being a single parent. Her daughter was born in 2008 and was diagnosed with ADHD, autism, a sensory processing disorder and PDA (pathological demand avoidance). Her son, born in 2009, was diagnosed with autism, low muscle tones and no spatial awareness. Both children have sleep disorders. The diagnosis of her children's conditions was a catalyst for change for Star. It was the birth of her son that started her determined journey to support other families.

Star was nominated for an Adult Learners' Week (now Festival of Learning) Award 2015 because she is a committed learner, a great ambassador for encouraging others to either return to learning or engage for the first time. Her personal progress bears little weight for her as her intention is to support others. During the past three years, Star has attended five Wiltshire Council community learning programmes and a workshop: Time 4 U, Budgets and Bargains, Cooking from Scratch, Family SEAL, an outdoors activity course and a family Circus Skills workshop. As part of the Cooking from Scratch programme, she has achieved the RSPH level 2 Award in Healthier Food and Special Diets. The carers' group has been running for three years and meets fortnightly. There is no screening for joining the group. Star ensures that the group is supportive to the families who attend as they are all aware of the demands that children who have similar conditions need. She also understands the pressures for families who have children with complex needs. The group is growing owing to Star's constant energy to ensure that families do not feel isolated. She is also actively engaging with other support networks to ensure that the members of the group receive relevant and appropriate information.

Star has been an important link for the Wiltshire Council Community Learning team. Initially, a Time 4 U course was organised for her group which was well attended owing to Star's persistence in encouraging the group to join. The group were apprehensive to enrol owing to having been out of learning for some time and had few or low qualifications. She helped with transport and became a link between the programme and the group. After the Time 4 U programme, she was determined to keep the learning going for the group. They identified a need for budgeting, as some of the learners receive benefits, so they ran Budgets and Bargains as a follow on course. Again, Star encouraged the group to attend. An opportunity arose to run a circus skills holiday activity in her area; Star advised about an appropriate venue which the families could access and she encouraged her group to attend. Star understood that the group needed some advice about cooking meals from scratch. They cooked together using their budgeting skills and created healthy, family meals. The course had embedded learning about nutrition so the group took the level 2 Award in Healthier Food and Special Diets.

It is evident that Star has been key for the group to both access and continue to learn together. She constantly uses social media, phone calls, cups of coffee, and offers a listening ear to reassure others that they don't have to feel isolated. She understands that if families have children with special educational needs, other families may not be keen to socialise. Star could not access an appropriate school place for her daughter for fifteen months. Without any local family help, this could have resulted in Star having to save her energy to manage at home. However, this created stronger links with the group. Her positive determination has enabled families to both learn and share separate time, away from home, in a supportive environment. Some of the group are now accessing Open University courses. The group will shortly gain charity status.

Star recognises that she is very determined to keep the learning momentum for both herself and others:

"It's the Cornish in me! I'm not prepared to accept a situation. I want to make it better. I want to empower others to be independent and not accept when there can be a solution if one is determined to find a way through."

What is Star's advice to others?

"Do it! Bite the bullet and don't be scared of the unknown."

Denise Hodgson

My name is Denise. I achieved Adult Senior Learner of the South West in the Adult Learners Week Awards 2010 (now Festival of Learning). I am now sixty-two years of age and still working full time at present as a lecturer at Yeovil College in Somerset.

When I was at school I was branded thick and often made to sit in the corner. At senior school the teachers treated me differently. They made me the class clown: making me read aloud, and allowing everyone to laugh when I got things wrong. One time the history teacher asked me to read aloud. We were learning about the Turks. I just wanted to melt into the ground and become invisible but even if I refused, it was made worse; I would be classified as a trouble maker. So, I read starting out well. Then I read, "the turkeys moved forward up the hill": the whole class burst into laughter but I was unsure why. I would leave crying and would cry every day before history and at home into my pillow. Every time I went into history class, the teacher would put up a picture of a turkey for the whole class to laugh at. This had huge implications for my self-esteem. I think I must have had depression as I look back now. I was at secondary school and took CSEs (Certificate of Secondary Education, as they were then) and went on to college to do catering. This was successful. Well, in the practical I got a distinction but the theory held me back. Still, no-one noticed my struggles. I worked in schools and hospitals in the kitchens for a good number of years. I had my babies and returned to catering. The shifts were helpful. Then the worst thing happened: my husband left after fifteen years of marriage. I was broken hearted, and used a lot of health and social care services. I survived a really dark time in my life. I had a fourteen year old and a two year old to bring up.

I wanted to provide for them so I got a job in care working with older people. This was good. I liked it and soon got promoted. Things were starting to improve. I then went to work with homeless people as a resettlement officer. I learnt a lot and started my Open University (OU) journey. Just after my first assignment my tutor contacted me and said my work was really good. I clearly understood the requirement but it was extremely fragmented. She said she thought I was dyslexic and wanted to send me for an educational assessment.

Well, this took place when I was approximately thirty-nine to forty-two. I can no longer remember, but the assessment came back and stated that I had a severe learning disability. I had no phonics. I cried a lot and was so emotional reading this account of me and then I realised why school was so hard and why I need to help others. Once I had the label it gave me support to help others to understand my learning needs. It is different for everyone. I had fifteen minute breaks in exams. With the OU I had an invigilator come to my house so I could sit the exam where I felt comfortable. I have a peach film and glasses to support my reading off white paper. In all exams I have a reader if I choose and fifteen minute breaks where I do stand up and walk around but like to do everything else myself. Since the Equality Act 2010 I have had another assessment as an employee. This was to support my need for the Dragon speech-to-text system and a laptop of my own. I have been asked to speak at local dyslexic clubs, which I have been delighted to attend. With my second course at the OU I had talking books which help my comprehension.

I never stop studying. I changed jobs a few times and then I was a manager in supported housing, working alongside people with mental health issues. From the Open University to counselling and group work, my educational pathway grew. I also trained to be a trainer and an assessor and verifier for the old NVQs. I was head hunted and became a training officer in a mental health trust. It felt strange as I still had a hard job to realise my knowledge and skills. This is still the case today.

I started work at Yeovil college approximately ten years ago after leaving the NHS with stress. I graduated as a teacher: cap and gown affair. This is how I won the Adult Learners Award (now Festival of Learning). Since then I have continued to study and grow. In my local community I have just become a finalist for a Pride Award in Somerset and Dorset's Unsung Hero. I am so very excited. The final date is this 4th December. The local housing group nominated me as an enthusiastic and inspirational teacher for teaching older people and young people in an intergenerational project for the past five years. It is such an honour.

I am a Lecturer in Health and Social Care at college and also hold a post of teaching and learning coach. This is about supporting other lecturers to develop creative teaching and positive risk taking. I only have two years left to work. My sons are both grown: one with a family of his own; the other son, the youngest, has his own business and works extremely hard. My mum used to help so much with child care, both when I was working and studying, while the boys were dependant.

I was a chair of a local organisation for seven years: interesting when my history teacher said I would never succeed or come to anything. I just wish I could see his face now!

Stewart Bell, Perth and Kinross Council

Personal Benefits of Reading and Writing

I looked 'dyslexic' up in my Chambers Adult Learners' Dictionary (not an easy word for me to find – it's hard when "y" replaces the vowel "i"!) and this is what it says, "A dyslexic person has difficulty in learning to recognise and form written words correctly." Well that sounds like me and indeed it is me.

I am very lucky and proud to be a member of the Letham Thursday night adult literacy group, which is a free class run by Perth and Kinross Council. Thursday night is one of the highlights of my week now. There are no tests or exams – it's all about the learners' needs and wishes. And so it's not like school or college in any way. One paid member of staff directs the group with the help of trained volunteers.

For the first twelve months of my learning experience I had one-to-one classes. I started by learning the sounds of each letter and then two-letter sounds. I was as slow as a snail and it was so hard and frustrating at times. I was then moved into a group. There we'd do a group warm-up and then split up to do one-to-one sessions. At this stage of my learning, I felt I was making real progress. I became as hungry as a bear and was coming on in leaps and bounds.

When you're an adult who can't read or write, it's hard! Because I look normal (maybe not what my mates say!) everybody just assumes you can. In a sad way I didn't miss what I never had. I had my ways of getting by. I just accepted it, got on with it and made the best of it. But I always wished I could read and write. Now I have learned to read, it is a joy and thrill in my life.

Here are just a few examples of how reading has helped me since I learnt, and, of course, what I missed out on all those wasted years. Buying a newspaper is something I've done every day since I started work at the age of sixteen over thirty years ago. I did so because that's what everyone else did, so I wanted to be the same. I looked at the pictures and tried to work out the stories that were illustrated by the pictures. After a bit, I started to recognise the easy words and kind of make sense of the articles in my own way.

My tutors have encouraged me to read books. They introduced me to Quick Reads and the Open Door series, which are written for adults but which are not over-long or particularly wordy. I have read quite a few now and have really enjoyed most of them. Time is my biggest enemy, however, when I'm reading! So I always keep a book in my jacket pocket in case I get a chance to dip in. A few years ago at my literacy class I, along with my fellow learners, was challenged to write a story on the subject of "A Day Like This" for the Scottish Book Trust. I wrote about my experiences as an adult literacy learner. When I am writing about myself it helps me believe in myself. And it showed on paper how much progress I was making.

One of the biggest benefits for me was being able to leave notes for my wife and kids and also writing down messages from phone calls. Before, I couldn't think about doing either. It was always a big problem for me. I couldn't write a note to Mary to tell her I'd gone out, where I was or what time to expect me home. Taking names and addresses over the phone was a nightmare. That nightmare has become a better dream. Another plus is being able to read instructions for myself, and not relying on someone else to do it for me. Medication was always a difficult one because that's something you can't really safely guess at, but I did sometimes! Other more obvious examples are form filling, raffle tickets, competition forms and so on where you have at a minimum to be able to write your name and address. When I'm out and about I can now read, and, more importantly, understand signs and directions. How important is that?

I used to have to kid on I was, for example, reading a newspaper when everyone else around me was reading theirs. You can get quite good at bluffing. More importantly for my sanity I don't have to be dishonest or lie about it any more. I feel in this regard that it has made me a better person and I am more comfortable in and with myself. One of my biggest thrills is being able to read what I want. A particular interest of mine is whisky. Tasting it (in moderation of course!) is what it's all about, but being able to read about the different types of whisky and its manufacture is a real thrill for me now. Now, I subscribe to two whisky magazines. I really enjoy reading whisky reference books. This has got me reading avidly at home. I now own about forty-five different whisky books and aim to add more. Only last week I pre-ordered a whisky book which will not be published for another four months. I can't walk past a book shop now without going in. And to think that not all that long ago I didn't even notice books or bookshops! To be honest I was scared of them.

And so my adult learning has helped me loads. From what I've recorded I hope you can see I feel different, something which has improved my life. I can't commend highly enough the people I've worked with (tutors and fellow learners), the methods used or the valuable material I've worked with. I really wish everyone with my experience could benefit the same!

Allison Churchill

I was born in south London, on the edge of Brixton in 1966. It was a wonderful multi-cultural melting pot of different faiths, ethnicity and class. I thought the whole world was like our neighbourhood, just like 'Sesame Street'. Our flat was on the seventh floor of a tower block where our game of 'chicken' was to hang by our fingers on the wrong side of the balcony whilst our friends punched our fingers.

We were considered 'posh' by many because my mother had worked as a switchboard operator and spoke 'properly' and that our father actually lived with us. Unfortunately, we wished he didn't as he was an angry and abusive man behind closed doors. My mother wouldn't leave him because she was too frightened that my sister and I would be taken away from her. She had two nervous breakdowns. Back then, we never knew who we would come home to after school, would it be happy mummy who would play board games with us, or angry mummy chasing us with a wooden spoon or crying mummy weeping on the sofa.

Our nan (dad's mum) lived with us in the early years, until she set fire to her bedroom the second time! Dad, mum, my sister and I slept in the other bedroom. Sometimes it was so cold we would sleep with hats and coats on in bed, drawing pictures in the ice on the inside of the windows.

When I went to secondary school I was considered 'common' because of where I came from. I thrived in the first year academically and was put up to the higher set the following year. But it was too hard for me and I never caught up. They advised for me to go down to the lower set again but my father refused, because I had embarrassed him. Consequently, I was put in to do eleven Ordinary Level exams (O levels) but left school with only two.

I joined a youth opportunities programme at sixteen years old and studied office work at a secretarial college, whilst doing work experience for a couple of different companies. I drifted from office job to office job for years, moving to Poole, Dorset when I was twenty-three. I lived with my sister to keep her company because her husband was in the RAF and she was lonely bringing up her little girl.

I was working in a toy shop when I met a young man. We went on to make a home together and had two sons. Sadly, our relationship fell apart. He had a couple of affairs, was unreliable with work and money and occasionally violent. The last straw was one evening he was going out again and my little boys begged him not to go. They stood on the front door step crying and I remember thinking to myself if he turns round to wave as he walks down the road, I'll give him another chance but he didn't. I thought to myself, hurt me all you like but you do not hurt them. This gave me the impetus to step up to the plate.

I saw in the local children's centre a course called 'maths for the terrified'. I thought, yep, that is me alright. I signed up for that and for a computer class for beginners. I really enjoyed these and they gave me the confidence to try more things. I ended up doing my City and Guilds 1, 2, 3 and 4 in maths (distinction) and eventually my GCSE (a high grade B). I couldn't believe I could do it, but I did! I carried on with computer classes, gaining in confidence and qualifications.

I took French classes for a few years (various education authorities), and I treated myself to doing lots of art classes (City and Guilds) too. I even obtained an A level in art which had always been my passion. I wanted to be a good example to my boys about studying and it seems to have worked. They both received really good GCSE results, my youngest son is doing his second year of A Levels and my eldest is in his first year at university. Proud mum! This is just one of the many things that adult learning has afforded me.

Thanks to my computer classes, I have a lovely job working at the maternity hospital on reception. I have made so many lovely friends through adult learning. I have gained in self-confidence. I even met my lovely husband on-line! We've been together for eleven years and married for five. He loves the fact that I am always busy and willing to try new things.

For the past two years, I have been a stalwart member of the New Bourne Community Choir (sponsored by the RCM) which brings me so much joy and lifts my spirits on the darkest of days. I am a member of the hospital craft club, which is a wonderful way of learning new skills in a fun environment. I have just passed my British Sign Language stage 1 qualification, partially paid for by the RCM.

I am now on the look-out for the next challenge! I can hardly believe how far I have come from the withdrawn, awkward and damaged child and teenager that I was. I am loving life and adult education has brought me so much of what is good in it. I recommend adult learning to everyone; it really can be life changing.

Anna-Lisa Egan

My grandma was a Warlpiri woman. She raised me when I was only about three years old at Waylilipa, which is sixty kilometers south from Yuendumu in the Tanami Desert of the Northern Territory of Australia. Her name was Jeannie Nungarrayi Egan. There were seven of us girls with our grandma and our grandfather. We all lived in a humpy before we had a house (a humpy is a shelter made of twigs and leaves). We lived on bush tucker. Our grandfather would come hunting too. He would drop all us girls off with our grandma and great grandma and we would look for goannas. My grandma and great grandma would go separate ways looking for fresh goanna tracks and dig a hole to find the goannas. They would get four or five goannas each. We would bring them back to our camp and cook them on the fire. In the winter my grandma taught all of us girls how to look for bush potatoes and honey ant.

The desert gets very, very hot and can be freezing in the winter. We had no electricity and no running water. My grandma spoke up for all that. She spoke up to the government and land council for us to get houses at Waylilipa, a water tank and a phone booth. She was strong and resilient. Never giving up on the outstation and looking after all of us girls in the bush at the same time.

My grandma was a teacher since 1974 who was well known as a strong and resilient leader in the Community of Yuendumu and Waylilipa. She worked as a teacher at Yuendumu School for thirty years. She always wanted a two way education for all Warlpiri kids around the Warlpiri region, which means learning about new ways but also keeping our culture and language strong. She even went to Chicago USA with her sister Bess Price, who is now a minister, and when she came back from America she was rewarded by Prime Minster Howard.

She was a loving and caring person who worried a lot about the kids wandering around at night and not coming to school, so after she retired she started a program in the year 2000, a program called Jaru Pirrijirdi, which means strong voices. This is a youth program which is run by the Warlpiri Youth Development Aboriginal Corporation. The program now runs football, basketball, softball and going out on bush trips and disco on weekends from 7:00pm to 10:00pm and opening the swimming pool every day for the kids.

I was proud of her, what she was doing and what she did and she always said to me education is a key. She is my role model and the most resilient person I know.

Toni Hodge, Swinburne University

Hope and determination

I was a person that was not given the chance of an education after the age of thirteen, so things seemed to deteriorate. My jobs were in pubs, factories, picking fruit and cleaning. I had children at a young age, a bad marriage that had violence, drugs and an alcoholic future. Then later to watch my child die.

So after I buried my youngest child, he was twenty-seven, I needed to find a way to cope with the pain and loss so I asked the government to send me to school: they agreed. So the Swinburne, Wantirna Campus was where I thought I would start this journey.

It was very hard for me to come to school, when I was still suffering from depression, suicide, anger problems, distrust and worst of all no faith in myself.

Not knowing if I would be able to stay in school at all, let alone be taught to read and write, I had days of such sadness, that I would either cry or get angry with my work projects and walk out of class.

I ended up asking for help both from the teachers and the school counsellor and psychologist and they came to my aid.

I have now been in school over three years and my whole outlook towards people and the system has got better. I have started writing short stories. I have now got to watch my second child slowly deteriorate and die from the same disease as my son died of. She is thirty-four.

If the school lets me return next year it may be the only way of handling this nightmare again. The teachers have been totally accepting of my circumstances and have done more than I ever could have foreseen to help me in my learning, and for that reason and my own determination, I have stayed in school, even though I may never work again as my age is a barrier. I will always say the best thing I ever decided to do in my life was going back to school. It really was the best thing I could have done.

Well, we all may chase rainbows, but the reality of learning: even a basic thing like reading and writing will make your rainbow easier to find.

Even though my pain and sadness will still come again and at times overwhelm me, though having these few years in school has made me feel more confident in how I handle the next part of my life, after the death of my next child.

School didn't give up on me even when everyone and everything else in the world did.

So thank you Swinburne!

Timothy Presser, Swinburne University

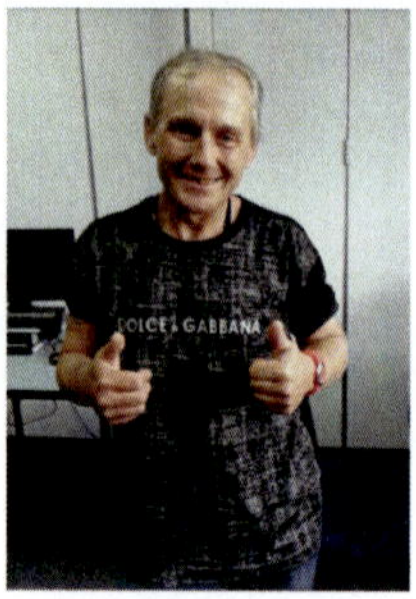

After a troubled youth, I dropped out of school at fifteen years of age. I came to Melbourne. A Salvation Army hostel had taken me in. The social worker helped me find a job in Sheet Metal and Engineering in Richmond, where unfortunately I started to take drugs.

I came down with depression after staying awake for nine days which cost me my job. I wanted an apprenticeship but was told I needed twelve months at night school.

My drug taking spiraled out of control, which led to hepatitis C, depression and eventually Acquired Brain Injury. I felt scared.

After years of detoxing and rehabilitation I decided it was time for me to get an education. So, I started at Swinburne in Prahran doing English, numeracy and computer skills. There were lots of barriers to overcome as I had not studied for thirty years. I could speak English but I did not know it. There were also lots of stops and starts due to my mental and physical health issues. However, I completed Certificate I of the General Education for Adults and then completed a number of units in Certificate II.

After a significant break I decided I needed to complete Certificate II to enable me to continue my education for work. I woke at 5:20am to leave home at 7:00am to catch the 7:18am train to Oakleigh, to change to the 693 bus to Stud Rd, and then change again to the 901 Airport bus to Wantirna, Swinburne. I arrived just before 8:30am. Tomorrow I am receiving my full Certificate II in General Education for Adults. This has taken six, long, hard, difficult but well worthwhile years. I feel great. I have achieved my goal.

Naseema Spaull, Swinburne University

My name is Naseema Spaull. I am thirty-eight years old. I come from India and English is my second language. I'm married to an Australian man, Adam, and have a child, Zechariah.

I was introduced to TAFE by a job provider when I was unemployed in 2010. I was terrified of going to TAFE because I thought that people might judge or discriminate against me because of my age. I was then thirty-three years old. Once I started as an introductory student, I was so surprised at the way teachers and students reacted towards me. They were extremely helpful and encouraging, able to make me feel comfortable and safe.

Before I started at TAFE, I did have a job at Coles where I worked for fourteen and a half years. However, I had to leave for personal circumstances and I wanted a change in my career.

The job provider gave me several options about careers but most work required some kind of skills, like English, maths and computers, which I did not have. Even though I speak English very well, my writing is not good enough. As a child, I did not have much of an education because where I come from, India, only rich children could afford to go to school.

At the age of eleven and a half years old, I was adopted by an Australian couple who gave me a second chance in life and the education I needed. When I started schooling here at primary and high school, I honestly did not enjoy the school because the students were so cruel and hurtful to me. At the time, I did not speak English very well and I had a funny accent which the students teased me about.

For years I struggled to be perfect with my English, especially with my writing and reading, even though I practised a lot by reading the newspaper or books and rewriting the texts into my own words. Also I am a chatterbox, so this helps with my spoken English.

I have mental, physical and alcohol problems which I have struggled with for many years and I still struggle with these. If it wasn't for my family and TAFE, who have given me the strength and support to carry on, I think I would give up. Also, their encouragement keeps me continuing to advance my education, where I'm gaining so much knowledge, skills and experience. I am improving a lot with my writing, reading and really getting better with computer programmes. I am learning how to cope with my life, juggling study and family commitments.

Now I am even writing a couple books about my son and my life with the help of the teachers, support workers and my husband.

Jasima Begum, City Gateway Women's Project

*Jasima's first name has been changed to protect her identity

I was born in Bangladesh and moved to England about five years after getting married. For me it was really difficult. I couldn't understand things. When I went outside, I was always scared because everything was completely new and there were only English people who I couldn't understand.

I became pregnant. We shared a room with some others, but after a while we became homeless. We then got a temporary house in Stepney Green. It was very hard, and I had a problem with domestic violence.

A few years later my daughter was diagnosed with leukaemia. It was so hard because I couldn't understand, I couldn't speak to the doctors properly and I wanted to know what was going on. I stayed with her in hospital for weeks. She had treatment over two years, and that's how I started to practice my English. My husband didn't help me at all. I was the one who always took her to the hospital. I had a second child too by then.

There was a lot of domestic violence. I can't explain how hard it was. Home didn't feel safe. And we were living on the ground floor and I was scared about being attacked by others too. Eventually in court they decided that my husband was not allowed to live with us. And then I heard about City Gateway.

I was always inside staying at home, depressed. I didn't know what to do. One of my friends told me I need to stop staying at home, telling me with my two children I couldn't stay in becoming more depressed as they have lives to live. My friend brought me to City Gateway and I signed up to ESOL class. I wanted to study because I needed to help my children and communicate with people in everyday life. I met so many different people on my courses – staff, volunteers and other learners helped me.

Life is a struggle if people don't know English here – it's really hard. If you don't know English it's like a barrier – you can't do anything and you can only speak to people who speak your own language. ESOL is really important for people – especially for women. They need to learn speaking, writing and reading. People who are born here can speak and read and write. But people born in other countries don't always know how. Many Bengali women just depend on their husbands and have no independence unless they can speak. It's also really important as a mother – if I couldn't speak English now I wouldn't understand half my children's conversations. I wouldn't know where they are going, whether they are talking about good things or bad things. I wouldn't be able to help them with their homework. It is so important.

I found ESOL was really good for me. It helped me with speaking, reading and writing. Before, I didn't feel comfortable to speak to people in the street or at the doctors or phoning the bank – now I can. And confidently. Before I would be scared to speak, and take a friend with me to the doctor to speak for me – now I go by myself. I am confident. I feel more independent.

My teacher was so good. I cannot say enough – she was wonderful. In one way she is my inspiration – she believed in me. She's the one who always noticed if I worried and gave me support. Lessons were fun, but it was difficult too because so much was going on at home it was difficult to concentrate on work. But City Gateway supported me. City Gateway is like a family. I felt happiness in the centre, people were so friendly – I'd see somebody's smiling face and be encouraged.

I like to meet new people! I like making friends from other cultures – all the friends I have now are from City Gateway. And City Gateway helped me with my personal life too. Oh, and Fran, she is really helpful. I love Fran! She helped me to speak to my social workers and to my lawyer. For legal things I need to really understand properly and speak exactly the right words in English, and Fran helped me get it right. And she helped me when sorting housing was difficult. City Gateway really know how to handle families and children.

I then went on to do parenting courses, Women's Voice (a public speaking and confidence course), and volunteering as a teaching assistant in ESOL. It was amazing! I feel proud of myself. Before, somebody was helping me study ESOL. And then there I was helping others in ESOL as a learning mentor. How can I say what it felt like… it was mind-blowing!

I am free to do what I want and go after my dreams – I want to care for disabled children one day, so I studied Childcare Level 1, maths and ICT with City Gateway to get closer to my goal. I love my job. I am meeting lots of new friends in the community and I am able to look after older people who don't have families with them.

Tutor Perspective

Jasima has also formed friendships at City Gateway and no longer feels isolated as she did when she first arrived in the UK. Fran, City Gateway's family support worker, took a lead on Jasima's safeguarding case and helped her deal with the difficult circumstances she was facing in her home life. Jasima has recently completed a focused writing course and plans to study Childcare level 2 in September in 2015 in order to move towards her career goal to work in childcare. In the meantime, in order to support her family and her studies, Jasima has recently secured work as a part-time health assistant in the community.

City Gateway Women's Project

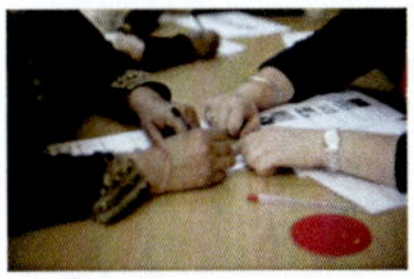

City Gateway Women's Programmes partners with marginalised and vulnerable women aged 19+ in East London to build confidence and skills, enabling every learner to become socially engaged and economically active.

We run free courses and drop-in activities in Poplar and Stepney, including ESOL, Lifeskills, Health Living programmes, Art sessions, Functional Skills English, Maths and ICT, Childcare, Volunteering Programmes, Employability, and Business Admin apprenticeships.

Our centres are friendly, busy places which welcome over 200 women each week - from a wide range of cultures and backgrounds. We also offer a free Information, Advice and Guidance service for women. You can expect to receive impartial and up-to-date advice in a friendly environment and help in overcoming any barriers to learning and progression.

Nurun Nahar Zorna Hoque, Idea Store Learning Whitechapel

My name is Nurun Nahar and my journey has been witnessed by all those around me; my transformation has been both physical and spiritual. The greatest part of my life is that I have grown a lot of confidence within myself. It is at times unbelievable for me because I always thought I would never come this far, but now I know that it is best to always carry on no matter what obstacles come in your way. This was a great motivation for me and will be in the future.

I started off by entering myself for the ESOL and Family Learning courses which helped me start the beginning of my great achievement. I then moved on to courses in IT, dance, and fitness. These courses made me feel much better about me. I have also tried my very best and encouraged other parents from my children's primary school, so I was quite happy to see other parents taking part in these courses.

It did take a lot of effort and commitment to get this far but I'd say it was worth it because now not only am I confident but I am able to see myself heading for a good future. I did have a difficult life during the first few courses due to my language barrier. I was not able to speak English or even understand much but these courses I have taken helped me improve on my language. I would say my understanding and speaking skills have improved a little. The other struggle was that I had to look after my children; this made me spend time on my family and not much time on my learning. However, it is all about working hard and really thinking of yourself as a strong person so you can do what you want and never let any obstacles stop you from getting where you want.

The way I overcame these issues was by taking more responsibilities, which meant that I had to focus well on my courses to prevent any more problems. Taking many courses and socialising with many different people helped me on my language barrier. I have attended nine different courses from February 2013 to January 2014. These courses included dance, IT, Aspiration for learner volunteers, specific dance classes for beginners and improvers, Computer Basics, Aerobics and many more. During these courses I attended a part time job as a shop assistant.

After that, I recently started full time in college and I am currently studying a Health and Social Care course, which means I have not yet finished it, so I still have some work to do. I am also part of a community organisation which allows me to hold events for women only.

'Adult learning' had a great impact on my life because now I am much more confident. I also think I have gained many skills as well as knowledge. Furthermore, adult learning helped me live through a good life and made it much easier for me. Many of my friends have asked about my achievements and were interested in some of the courses I have taken, so some of them decided to join adult learning.

In the year 2014 I received the National Individual Award and Learning in Families and Communities Award from Adult Learners Week (now Festival of Learning). I have gotten this far due to my hard work and overcoming any fears and obstacles. Also I had a lot of support from a special member called Jasmine Hossain who works in the Idea Store library. I got many nominations to get this award and I am very grateful for everyone who supported me and everyone who thought of me as an inspiration. I would like to see many people who are interested in adult learning to take part and become successful.

Experiencing these courses, socialising and receiving awards was surprising and I am glad to say that I am proud of myself for getting this far.

Tutor Perspective: Jasmine Hossain

I had a feeling that Nurun would have an inspirational story to share, but I had no idea that she would just blow me away. Nurun has been with Idea Store Learning since 2005, but she does not generally talk much about herself. When I heard Nurun's 'behind the scene' story, for me, it actually magnified her personal achievements and I could see immediately that she was an inspiration for others, as I felt inspired myself.

I remember listening and thinking that Nurun's challenges were 'huge' for her, but at the same time she was not unique. Lots of people react differently when faced with challenges, but what Nurun did was to actually re-invent herself and become the person she needed to be to survive the storm in her life. She did this magnificently through hard work and dedication. She invested in herself by embracing learning to better herself. She reflected on the aspects she needed to change for herself and she just focused on them and achieved her goals. Her ultimate motivation was to be in a position to better support her children and to be the role model that she wanted to be, so Family Learning literacy and numeracy were high on her agenda.

The Nurun that first joined the 'Volunteering in your child's school' (delivered by Idea Store Learning) in 2005 was very shy and nervous, and you might not even have noticed her because she spoke very little, but over the years Nurun has transformed and now she is a much slimmer, more radiant, more confident, bubblier, happier and younger looking Nurun who converses in English. She transformed right in front of our eyes and we all saw it happen.

Nurun's literacy, numeracy and IT tutors all thought that they knew her, but they had no idea just how many courses she was doing and indeed how varied they were. In fact, some tutors had no idea about the dance and fitness courses, all that they noticed was that Nurun appeared more confident. Nurun was proud that she had lost 10kg and gained a job within a year. The confidence boost that she got from the weight-loss was important for her. Who would have thought that the best way to improve your language, literacy and IT skills is by joining a dance and/or fitness course!

Listening to Nurun's story made me feel like I was putting a jigsaw together and finally I could see all the pieces that together made up the bigger picture of the real Nurun Nahar Zorna-Hoque. I hope that others will also be inspired to make a difference in their lives through learning.

Idea Store Learning

Idea Stores are more than just a library or a place of learning. As well as the traditional library service, they offer a wide range of adult education classes, along with career support, training, meeting areas, cafes and arts and leisure pursuits.

After the largest consultation exercise ever undertaken by Tower Hamlets Council, the Secretary of State for the Department of Culture, Media and Sport, launched the groundbreaking Idea Stores concept in April 1999. Tower Hamlets unveiled its plans to invest £20 million in library and learning services at a time when the national trend was to decrease funding. The idea became a reality in May 2002 when the first, prototype Idea Store opened at Bow. This was followed by Idea Store Chrisp Street in July 2004, Idea Store Whitechapel in September 2005, Idea Store Canary Wharf in March 2006 and Idea Store Watney Market in May 2013.

With open, flexible spaces, with lots of glass and natural light, and cafes with lovely views over cityscapes, the opportunity to enjoy a yoga or salsa dance class, or any of the 900 courses offered yearly, contributes to a quality library and learning experience. Idea Store Learning provides a range of courses to adult learners to support their ambitions to improve their skills, help their families, have fun and make a positive contribution to the local community.

Tower Hamlets Council is committed to keeping learning affordable for everyone. In partnership with the Skills Funding Agency we are able to offer reduced fees on many programmes for those most in need. With maths and English, an ever increasing requirement for employment and further education, we offer a number of free programmes to help residents along their way and achieve their absolute potential. Many of the programmes are offered within the Idea Stores themselves and provide an opportunity to access online learning, books and a range of other free activities that will inspire.

Our tutors are experts in their fields and as such offer the best learning experience. Inspiring and passionate, many of them continue to work in their occupations and so will provide you with the most current knowledge and skills. Student satisfaction with our service is outstanding. Idea Store are proud to say that 92% of all learners judge their experience to be good or excellent.

Margaret Green, Bradford College

My name is Margaret Green. I am fifty-two years old and employed as a Supply Chain Lead for the Materials Management Department (procurement) at the Calderdale and Huddersfield NHS Foundation Trust.

I began working at the NHS 10 years ago in the Laundry department; I stayed there for two years and was successful in gaining a role in the pharmacy department. This opened up a lot of opportunities for me, one of which was to participate in gaining up-to date-qualifications. This was something that I was very apprehensive about due to my past experiences.

The qualification was an Intermediate Apprenticeship in Pharmacy Services. This included completing NVQ, BTEC, employment and Key Skills (English and maths level 1). I chose to enrol on a NVQ as it was work based and would enhance my knowledge and improve my confidence. I have always felt that I was never very academic and thought I would really like to have up-to-date relevant qualifications which I feel would enhance the skills I had obtained throughout my past career.

NVQs also appealed to me as I was informed that I would have a personal assessor to talk me through any queries or concerns. This was very important to me as I did not have very much confidence in myself and felt very unsure of my abilities. I also felt very reassured as I was aware it would not include an exam at the end and I could work through things at my own pace. This suited my style of learning as, at the age of fifty-two, going back into an education setting was well out of my comfort zone.

At first I was a little daunted by the amount of computer use but with the guidance of my assessor, Nicola Crawley, I now use my home computer with much more confidence. Using the Ecordia system was a very good way of recording my course work. It was easily retained and I could refer back to previous work quickly. It was a good system and easy to find my way around and meant I did not have to have lots of paper work that could have been lost or destroyed easily. This has now allowed me to be confident enough to apply and be successful in gaining my present position, which involves a great deal of computer based work and knowledge, something that I once thought above me. I feel I have really acquired many skills whilst studying this NVQ. The qualifications I received when I completed the course have opened many more doors to me.

The personal impact it has had has been very positive and the feedback I received from my assessor was very encouraging as she always stated how well I had researched things. I really enjoyed gathering the information and spent many hours researching some of the information required to complete the course work. I feel it took a great deal of work to complete my course work to a standard that I felt happy with. It was not always easy. There were times I cried over it and felt that my work was not good enough, but my assessor Nicola was always there reassuring me that the work I was producing was to a very high standard. Her encouraging words kept me going. I worked most evenings and at weekends I would work day and night putting my heart and soul into the course.

My family and my assessor were extremely supportive and patient with me whilst I completed the course, and continue to support me in my new role as Supply Chain Lead. I would not have been able to apply for this role if I did not have the relevant qualifications. My families have informed me that they have noticed a change in my confidence levels and my ability to study and research. My sons are impressed with my computer skills now!

In my new role I have more responsibilities and I am now responsible for a team of nineteen staff and work across two sites. Part of my role involves recruiting staff into our department. I am able to use my skills and knowledge to assist individuals who may come across with low self-esteem and confidence issues to overcome their barriers and I now encourage them to see their own ability just as my assessor did for me.

After being told to stand on a chair in front of the class while a teacher informed everyone in the class that I was not worth teaching and would never amount to anything, I now feel I have really accomplished something. I am so proud of myself and looking forward to continuing with my new challenge: not bad for someone who grew up with low self-esteem and confidence issues.

Many thanks to my assessor Nicola and Bradford College for seeing potential in me that I had long ago forgotten I had. Words cannot express my thanks and gratitude to them for my new found confidence. I really could not have done this without her.

Overall, I can say that I would recommend an NVQ to anyone who wishes to gain qualifications but, most of all, that it most definitely improves knowledge of the job that you are undertaking and confidence, no matter your age or your perceived ability. The help and assistance is there, you just have to have the courage to step out of your comfort zone and accept the support to grow your future.

<u>Tutor Perspective: Nicola Crawley</u>
Senior Education and Training Pharmacy Technician, Calderdale and Huddersfield NHS Foundation Trust

The Intermediate Apprenticeship in Pharmacy Services was mandatory for Margaret's pharmacy role. Margaret was extremely apprehensive about this and began the course a very nervous and anxious learner. She did not believe she had the capabilities to complete the course, especially on hearing of all the different elements including IT and numeracy skills. As we worked together on the course it was clear that many of Margaret's learning barriers were due to previous negative learning experiences. She put her all into the course and it was extremely rewarding as an assessor to see her confidence grow. So much so that she went on to complete the

Distinction sections of the BTEC element. I believe Margaret was always very capable. She just needed the confidence. She overcame her barriers that had prevented her from progressing to her full potential for so long. I am very pleased that I was part of her journey in achieving her goals and true potential.

.:] Terry Easter, City Lit

Multimedia

An audio interview between Terry Easter and Tara Furlong is available on http://rapal.org.uk/resilience/, with accompanying transcript.

Terry's Story

My name is Terry Easter. I am fifty-three years of age and I work for Thames Reach as a support worker. Thames Reach is a homeless charity which has projects over the south of England including hostels, supported housing, an employment academy and it also offers a floating support service to continue to support service users when they have moved into independent accommodation.

Four years ago I was living in supported housing which was run by Southwark council after years of living rough on the streets of London and various short stay hostels. I found myself in this position after a long period of alcohol abuse. I left school at the age of fifteen without any qualifications; finding work was a lot easier than it is today when I left school.

When I was in supported housing I was introduced to Maggie Sandy, who is a Resettlement Officer at Southwark council and I began working with alcohol misuse workers and went into residential detox. When I returned from detox I needed to do something meaningful to help me stay sober and try to move on with my life.

I applied to take a peer mentor course with New Direction, which is an alcohol and substance misuse service. After being clean for six months, I was accepted to take the course which ran for three months and I attended four days a week. Not only did this keep me occupied, it gave me the confidence to engage more and helped with my future learning as there was a lot of written work to be completed. If I am honest, I was surprised to pass the course and I was allocated a voluntary placement with New Direction, which I enjoyed and, looking back, it provided me with the confidence and experience to move forward with my continued learning.

Maggie Sandy told me about Thames Reach, as she was previously employed by them, and gave me the details of the apprenticeship scheme they run. She encouraged me to apply and helped me with the application and provided me with a reference.

I had my doubts about applying especially when I learnt I would have to attend college once a week for a year and gain a qualification. I had not been in a classroom since I was fourteen, other than the peer mentor course, which was pretty laid back and did not involve using a computer, which I was very apprehensive about as I had never been near a computer in my life.

Again I was surprised when I was interviewed for the apprenticeship scheme and was successful but I still had apprehensions about attending college as I thought at my age it was much too late. But with much encouragement from Maggie Sandy and the tutor at City Lit College, Lucy Robson, I decided to give it my best and see what happened but I have to admit I was not very hopeful of being successful in gaining the qualification needed to obtain employment. I had plenty of life experience but the thought of being in a classroom and using a computer was daunting.

I can not praise Lucy Robson enough. She showed great patience with me and, when I became frustrated as I thought I was not coping, she assured me I was doing ok and took time to discuss any problems I was having. I started to meet with some of the other students of a weekend and we went over the assignments we were set. They also helped me with learning around the computer and I found I was really enjoying learning and using a computer which, was something I honestly thought I would never say.

I managed to pass and gain my qualifications in health and social care as well as English and maths, which I would never have thought possible. Going to college and learning was one of the best decisions I ever made and it was enjoyable and has given me the confidence and attitude to try anything. I now know that age is no barrier to learning. I also feel my voluntary work with new direction was a great starting point and would recommend voluntary work for anyone thinking of a change as it is a great way of gaining experience.

Amy Gaskin, Derbyshire County Council Adult Community Education Service

I come from a travelling family and we were always moving about. So, I never went to school as a child, and I never learned to read or write at all.

When I started my family, I stopped travelling because I wanted my children to be brought up with the chance to read and write, to see that they could do it.

Then when they started to come home with homework, it was horrible: I had to tell the school that I couldn't help them with it, because I couldn't read or write. Compared to when I was a child, you do get more people today who are sympathetic, but I still felt like a lot of people were looking at me as if it was my fault and that I should be able to do something about it: it's not a nice feeling.

But I was pleased that my children had the opportunities I hadn't; that they could get the skills to get a job. I was so proud when one of my sons went to college and qualified as a farrier: it was such an achievement for a travelling lad! And they can help their children with their school work.

I wanted to be able to read and write, but for a long time I never got round to doing anything about it for myself. I used to just get by, to pretend. I'd bluff my way through everyday situations – if I was in a shop and I found I had to read something I'd say stuff like I'd forgotten my glasses and ask could they read it to me – you get good at covering up. Today, there is a form to fill in for everything you do – I'd have to get my daughter to help me with stuff that I needed to read and write.

It affects every part of your life. For example, the other day I was in the supermarket and I'd accidentally unloaded my shopping in an aisle that was for hand baskets only. One woman was really nasty about it, even when I explained that I hadn't been able to read the sign, and everyone was looking at us.

You feel stupid when you can't read and write like everyone else but you just try to blank it out. I tried once to start to learn, when my boys were little, but the classes were too big for me. And then as you get older, it can get harder and harder to do something about it. But just over a year ago, at my son's school, I met a woman who said she had been going to adult education classes to get help with her reading and writing. I thought, "why not try?" and I found myself phoning up to find out more.

I've been going for over a year now and I really do like it. At first I was shy, and I felt very nervous – I remember going up in the lift to my first class and being scared that everyone would be so much better than me. But the classes are a nice size and the two tutors are understanding. You can talk to them about anything, and they know that with me they are starting from the basics, but they have time for you. I said to myself, "I'm going to stick at this", and I'm glad I have, because I like it.

My little granddaughter had been begging me to read to her: she was always pushing books at me. My tutor suggested I brought in one of her story books, and we practised until I felt confident enough to read the story to her. Then I did the Reading Agency's 'Six Book Challenge' through class. I'd never been in a library before but I liked going with the class, and they told us that reading books to children, or recipes, or poetry and so on could all count towards the six things we needed to read. I took out six books – children's books like 'Mog the Cat' and 'Fox's Socks'. I really liked reading them, so I then took out six more.

We'd also talk in class about what we'd read. I enjoyed that. I remember so often when I'd be collecting my children or grandchildren from school the other mums would be talking about what they'd read and I wouldn't be able to join in the conversation.

The best thing has been being able to make my granddaughter happy when I read her a story, but it has also been really exciting, finding that I recognise the words on the page and that I know what they mean. Even words like 'the' or 'dog': it feels incredible, and to me it's a really big thing, so I'm definitely going to keep going.

I'm taking things one step at a time, but I've always wanted to get a Catherine Cookson book and be able to read it: I've always listened to everyone saying how good her books are, so I'd like to see if I can read one. And at some point I'd also love to learn how to use a computer. My son has got an iPad and he gets so much out of it – he can even get music that was played when I was a teenager and listen to it – I think it could open up a whole world of possibilities.

I feel like a new, more confident person now. I'm proud of myself for going to classes and sticking at them. And when I finished the Six Book Challenge and got my certificate, well can you imagine how I felt? I'd never been to school or got any qualifications, so it felt really good!

If you are feeling embarrassed or worried about your reading and writing, there are places where you can go and ask for help. You've just got to find that first little bit of courage to take the first step.

The Reading Agency 'Reading Ahead'

Everything changes when we read. This is the belief that underpins the activity of The Reading Agency, a national charity that has a vision for a world where everyone is a confident and enthusiastic reader. Working with all ages and abilities, it creates and delivers innovative reading opportunities which inspire more people to read more; encourages them to share their enjoyment of reading with others and celebrate the difference that reading makes to all our lives. Among these are Reading Ahead (formerly the Six Book Challenge), the Quick Reads publishing initiative and World Book Night, all of which involve public libraries, colleges, adult community learning, prisons and workplaces in reaching out to people for whom reading is a struggle or who don't see themselves as readers. The discovery that reading can be a pleasure is transformational for many, opening doors to new worlds or simply changing everyday life.

Judy McGuire, TasTAFE

Boulder Hopping

My name is Jasmine and I have lived in Tasmania all my life. I have diabetes and I live near the beach with my partner and two cats. This story is my story about my contribution to resilience; where, what, how and why. So, please join me.

I was born in 1968, in the Royal Hobart Hospital and I had two younger brothers who I did not know about until later on in life. I was placed into foster care at the age of three years. I was then placed into a foster home and I lived there until I was twelve years old. It was then that I was returned to my biological family. The situation in my foster home was that my foster parents had their own daughter who was a year older than me. It happened sometimes that I was mean to her even though she was always lovely to me. After I had been with them for two years they adopted twin girls who became my sisters. In the end I had three sisters on my foster parents' side and two brothers on my biological side.

When I returned to my mother and brothers, she had remarried. I found that I did not really get on with her very well. After a few years of living there, it was obvious to me that this situation was why I had gone into care in the first place. My mother was very abusive towards her children. I was kicked out of home because of my sexuality. I lived on the street, where I had to learn how to defend myself or get bashed up. It was at this time that, unfortunately, I got into drugs and alcohol and joined up with some friends who encouraged me in my drug use. It was at this time that I did not want anything to do with my mother.

I felt I was a failure and my attitude to life had changed but I did not know how. I did not really care for anyone. I did not even like myself. Life was a bit of a joke for me and I did not want to deal with my life in general and I used people to get what I wanted.

One of the ways I tried to break out of this was by being involved with the Army Reserves here in Hobart. The end result of all of this was to cause communication breakdowns between myself and other people around me. I then spent a lot of years just stuffing around and did not really achieve anything in my life or my state of mind. There were times when I did go forward but I continually got knocked down and I could not help myself or the others who were around me.

I think the worst time of my life was getting into trouble with the law and not realising that I had done anything wrong. I was thirty-seven years old and lived in Launceston at the time. It was at this time that I spent six months in prison and lost my job and everything I owned and my friends. Most importantly, it was at this time that I lost my respect for myself and life in general. I knew before I went to prison that I was suffering from depression and then later on I was diagnosed with PTSD (Post Traumatic Stress Disorder). The one good thing about my time in prison was that it did teach me that I had to take responsibility for my own actions. I did learn from this and try and move forward on my release. I was able to stay at my foster dad's place. This was not easy for me and I found this hard and I did not really cope very well. I think this was because I was still having things that came up in prison pressing on my mind. One example of this is that when it was medication time we had to line up for it and I would relive this in my mind. Another example would be when I remember the feeling of how I reacted to the wake up call or to lock down at 6.50pm every night. I would remember how it felt hearing the cries of other inmates who had just come in or who were just having a bad day.

My life only started to change for the better when I began to look at study as an option in my life. My motivation to come back to study was to further my education. I knew for some time that I needed help with my maths and English. It was a great help but the biggest benefit was from doing Certificate IV in Mental Health. This is an area that I have been passionate about because of my experience of living with PTSD. For a long time I have had to deal with symptoms and signs of this. By doing the certificate I have been helped a lot. It helped me to come to terms with the shock when I found out (when I was thirty-eight years old) that my father had taken his own life. I could not really understand this but I learnt to talk about my issues as I wanted to get on with my life. I talked about my PTSD in my mental health course and this showed me how valuable it was to talk about it. I also had the strong motivation that I would not be a nobody. I could then acknowledge my difficulties and really move forward. This is the heart of the matter for me because it is that resilience and getting back self-esteem through counselling that has given me a renewed life. I now want to learn and seek help to find out why and what I did to end up in prison. In this way I have gained self-esteem and I can now take one day at a time and leave behind my feelings of shame.

When I was a young girl my actual dream was to be an Australian soccer player: not surprisingly that went pear shaped. It was only when reading my welfare files when I was twenty years old that I decided that I wanted to be a social worker. It was different issues in my life which turned that upside down. I had no support from family, or love or support or encouragement in my life. It was hard and I thought I would just turn out like my mother.

My setbacks in my life were difficult, such as prison, self-doubt and low self-esteem. When I went to prison the things that really stood out for me were the things I mentioned before. The things that I knew I needed were like a job, a relationship with family, friends, my car, all my belongings and my dignity.

I can see now that self-talk played a big part in my setbacks. I felt everyone around me was watching and I could not get through that. Even when people said that I was okay, I had a real negative vibe around me. It showed up because I did not have a lot of friends around me any more. I was still feeling ashamed and I continued to see my counsellor and do workshops on how to cope with things that really pissed me off. I worked on how to deal with what I did and how to move forward from the situation I was in.

Well, I did overcome my setbacks. I took responsibility for my own actions. I took one day at a time. I learnt to love me. I found that others were changing my own attitude. I had a willingness to move on. In time I enrolled in a course and sought some counselling and showed a willingness to move on with my life.

By using the tools I had learnt in counselling and with self-talk involved, I began to communicate with my family who wanted to be around me. It was then that I started to move forward by respecting myself and encouraging myself to be honest with myself and others. It was by putting myself first and loving those around me that I could stay focused and not get back in the wrong mind set again like before.

I have come a long way and I continue to go forward now more than backwards in my life. It's now 2015 and I have achieved so much like not getting into trouble with the law. That is a thing of the past now. Now that is how it is going to stay this year and always. I have managed to do a Certificate in Mental Health First Aid and Certificate IV in Mental Health and maths and English through TAFE. I have been a volunteer with St John Ambulance and a driver also. I also now have a permanent relationship. My goal is to go to university next year. One day I will be doing what I always wanted to do, working as a social worker.

I have applied for university and I am waiting to hear back but I have put it in motion. So, if you're thinking about doing training or education: stop procrastinating and get on with it!

"Always remember that your present situation is not your final destination. The best is yet to come."

Kym Ivory, Churchill Education

I have been married for twenty eight years and am a mum of four of a blended family. I have nine grandchildren, whom I adore. I have had many different jobs, including a full time tip truck driver, a head cook in a cafe, a vocal coach, mentor/counsellor, kitchen hand, shop assistant, choir instructor, producer, director, motivational speaker and events organiser to name a few. I love looking after my grandchildren and nurturing their future. I love to write and am in the process of writing my first book. My passion right now is to become qualified to work in the education arena and help as many children as I can to realise their dreams and aspirations, no matter how big they are, to materialise.

The journey so far...

I didn't make it at high school past year 11 and did VCE year 12 at a TAFE college in Geelong. I failed miserably and wound up pregnant and lost. It was years before I recovered enough to stand tall. Back then I was seventeen. As I look back at fifty-two, I find the struggles and journey worth every step it took to climb out and I don't think I would change anything.

I began to volunteer at Lifeline and became a telephone counsellor. I kept training and became a facilitator and began to train others to answer calls from people in crisis, hardship, loneliness, loss and grief. It was so rewarding. I felt like I was giving something back to a society that, although didn't necessarily understand my situation as a single mum in 1981, did gear me up to help. It geared me up to help those I trained to understand that people come from different walks of life and our job was never to judge but to listen and respect those in need.

We moved to another state because of hardship ourselves and I was faced with the prospect of home-schooling our daughter. Another journey began. It was a tough decision because I would be responsible for her education. I second guessed myself many times before finally embarking on this epic journey. It turned out to be the best thing we ever did. To see her being harassed at school and failing miserably, to becoming an independent, self reliant, compassionate, intelligent communicator who owns and runs two businesses and has employed over twenty-five staff in fifteen years, who is now Australia's first remedial massage business coach, is proof to me that I made the right decision. It's not for the faint hearted and I planned much of her education around teaching her how to learn. She is still learning, and has two of her own children now.

Along the way, I had the privilege of being asked to mentor two boys at the same secondary college. One whose mother had died when he was fifteen and he himself had an eye disorder that would send him blind by the time he was twenty. The other was a bright thirteen year old who struggled to articulate his ideas when doing English assignments. The fifteen year old was closed and grieving both his mother's death and the prospect of never having a licence, seeing his children or being independent. It was really hard at first. Our conversations were short and closed. It seemed nothing could unlock him. I kept at it, knowing that there had to be something that would connect us. I found it in a trip he had taken with his dad a few months earlier. After six weeks together in a room filled with awkward silences, I brought along my year ten photos of a trip to Ayers Rock (Uluru) and showed him. He looked at them and a smile appeared on his face (at my expense of course) at the sight of the photos from the seventies. We found common ground and he began to slowly but surely unpack his trip with me. We made it into a report complete with photos. I never gave up on the task I had been given. It was an exciting day. We then moved to classes he liked in the next weeks and months including textiles and IT. Life had found him and I was honoured to share the journey back with him.

The thirteen year old came to me in such an anxious state. He could read, write and speak well about what he had read but when it came time for the written assignment, he floundered. His teacher at the time was just impatient and there was no time to 'wait' for him. His assignment was due in the next few days and he was a mess. We got out those questions and he answered every one of them and I wrote down the answers word for word for him. He then wrote it all out in his own handwriting and then handed it in the following day. When I saw him the following week, he was so excited to tell me that he had passed!! All I had to do was believe in him. That's all he needed. I was with him for another term and learned so much about his life and we directed learning around what he loved and it worked. Always keep going, try new things, take risks, never give up.

In recent years, because of my love for singing and my passion for music, I became a vocal coach and taught in my little home town. I wanted to bring something to my community that was otherwise inaccessible apart from a long drive. I taught and mentored children for three years from my home and then began to go into schools to teach basic vocal, choir and stage presence. I wrote a six week program and have run it with great success twice now in the local primary school. From that program I was asked to write, direct and produce the end of year school concert. It was a wonderful success and from that came a job to teach it to the whole school. The teachers discovered a creativity in some of their students that they had never seen before. I was overwhelmed. I have never had formal training and so this year I decided to do something about that and began a Diploma of Education Assist. I thought I could do so much more with a qualification to help children develop their hidden gifts and talents that would lead to them becoming confident, independent, resilient, capable, strong adults who would know who they are and want to contribute to society like I have had the privilege to do so often in my life.

Mustafe Nor, TAFE Brisbane

My family were lucky to escape...

I was born in Hargeisa, the capital city of Somalia. Both my parents are Somalis too. I have five sisters and four brothers. When I was five years old, a war began in Somalia. People started to leave the country because it was no longer safe. My family were very lucky as we were able to move to New Zealand. I lived there for seven years.

When I was a young boy in New Zealand, I couldn't focus at school. I would always get in trouble because I was playing around and not listening. I would get in trouble at home, at school, and everywhere. I was kicked out of many schools. I was fighting all the time and breaking windows of homes and cars. I was too much to handle for anyone. I even went to juvenile detention for a week. My mum and dad decided to send me back to Somalia to live with my grandma. There were several reasons for this. If I misbehaved in New Zealand, I would not get into much trouble. In Somalia the schools are strict and teachers hit students if they misbehave or get something wrong. I could also learn about my religion, Islam.

After nine years in Somalia I came to Australia. I now study in the Skills for Employment and Education (SEE) course at TAFE Queensland, Southbank. I also work on weekends at a fruit shop, where I do odd jobs and help stack the shelves. The SEE course is for adults who need help with their English speaking, reading and writing and maths. I decided to participate in SEE because most of the people that go there are adults and they respect you for who you are. There are many people from different religions and backgrounds. There are Christians, Jews, Muslims, Hindus and people of no faith, yet we all get along.

TAFE Queensland is great. I have made many good friends. My teachers like me because I am a good student and my teachers are really kind. My reading and writing is improving day by day. I now have confidence to talk to anybody. I would advise other adults or teenagers who dropped out of school to further their education. It is vital to have faith in yourself so that you can make great things happen. I am studying hard and try my very best to achieve my dreams because I want to become a professional football coach. I have adapted well to TAFE Queensland. Thanks to what I have learned there, I have a job and am now earning money and sending some to my grandma. I want her to know that I haven't forgotten her.

I have also learned that if you keep dreaming and believing you can go far. Education is also important. Whether you are old or if you are young, I believe through education we can change our world for the better.

Amanda Derry

My Recovery Story

I was introduced to the WEA (Workers Educational Association) and Endurance creative writing class in Hoole Community Centre, Chester in 2009, run by Tina Scriven. The Endurance organisation, which is a partner organisation with WEA, was started by a member in the AA Fellowship and supports people addicted to alcohol and drugs. Endurance developed to include adults with depression and emotional problems (like me), to encourage them back to learning with new skills, career opportunities and to feel more confident about their personal and learning abilities.

Having been fortunate to be in the education system all my life, I went onto Higher Education after school and college. I had to leave two degree courses due to nervous breakdowns, but completed the third degree which I was accepted on. My last breakdown completely overtook me. I was committed to hospital for a month and had to leave my workplace. I put a lot of pressure and blame on myself. When I joined the WEA class, I had no self confidence, had ceased all my interests and only saw close family, and friends intermittently. I had no confidence in my writing abilities either: I'd always enjoyed the process of reading and writing, but my breakdown left me feeling I had nothing to offer. I felt accepted within the class. I made friends with a student, Alan, and he mentored me, encouraging me to write and socialize more. I gradually began to write stories and poetry about my family background and experiences. I felt each piece of writing formed a jigsaw piece, so each time I placed one down I understood more about myself. I wrote about my grandmother and identified with the isolation and depression she felt. I began the process of writing a book about my family background and how their experiences have been passed down in different generations. I explored alcoholism in my family and how we'd been affected by it. My mum came to the classes and I understood her more as a person, not just a parent.

The creative writing class started an allotment venture: we wrote a poem based on it, which I read out in a Hoole Endurance and WEA awards ceremony. The allotment became a spiritual home for me, as I coaxed Alan, who had health problems, to walk down the road where we met Tina. We fought the obstacles that faced us in the allotment, until we achieved a semblance of order and success.

As well as the creative writing class, I received support from the hospital, care in the community, my family, friends and husband. I also joined WEA through people I met in the class, which is a group aimed at people with emotional problems. For me, working the twelve step program provided a stability and way of living that enabled me to realize short and long-term goals.

The confidence I developed, through being part of a community class and committing myself to it every week, encouraged me to apply for voluntary work in St. John's church, which led me to work with another church, St.

Peter's. I started to run a voluntary arts and crafts workshop in the church within a supportive well-being group called 3rd Space, by utilizing my artistic background to help draw out students' innate creativity. In the same way that writing can be a cathartic, imaginative process, I view art as therapeutic and enjoyable. I've also been able to drive again. I visit family around the country on train, I went on holiday abroad and intend to travel more in the future. I have developed strong family and social networks and live a satisfying and varied life.

I gained certificates in the WEA and Endurance creative writing, and even joined a community choir which was set up in Hoole, through the class. Tina asked if I could help teach students in her writing classes, utilizing my literacy skills. This led me to being employed as a WEA support tutor. I can identify with learners with disabilities which make them feel isolated or who experience confidence and emotional problems; which are often associated with learning difficulties. I achieved the PTTLS initial teaching qualification through WEA and I enjoyed going back to studying. This qualification was an introduction to teaching adults in community learning, which is a direction I'm following after trying to find a meaningful vocation for years. I next completed a level 2 teaching adults' basic skills qualification at Deeside College.

My tutor Tina nominated me for NIACE (now Learning and Work Institute, Festival of Learning) Student of the Year and I was awarded the WEA Regional North-West winner, which was a really good but unexpected surprise! I attended the WEA national awards ceremony in Birmingham's Custard Factory, which was a great experience: also the first time I'd properly visited

Birmingham. The other students and groups nominated for awards seemed very outstanding and I felt honoured that I'd been considered accomplished enough to achieve the award.

Not long after gaining the WEA award, I was telephoned by a learning manager in Manchester, Catherine Kay, who was looking for a tutor to teach a new Ascentis course and I had been recommended by my PTTLS tutor. I accepted the role and successfully finished teaching my first course recently, as well as helping out with the course at another venue. This September I'm starting my arts class in St. Peter's as a paid WEA tutor, and will be commencing two other classes in Manchester teaching the Ascentis course.

Because of my positive experiences as an adult learner, I would support anyone who was thinking of starting a new course, especially in community learning. If they are concerned about starting a course because they haven't felt they belonged in formal education, I would reassure them that community learning is much more inclusive to individual needs and accessible: centres where learning takes place are often easier to travel to. I also believe that adults can learn at any age and the process of self-development and progress never ends.

Lindsay Cussons, WEA

I hadn't heard of WEA before I started attending their classes. The previous adult learning class I'd taken part in was a French course at Chester University, which I found stressful because it was too academic and formal for me.

I found out about WEA when I went to St Peter's Church in Chester. Everyone seemed friendly and I started talking to Amanda (Derry) who asked if I'd like to join a drop-in art class she was starting up within the church. When I was young I thought I was hopeless at art because I felt discouraged by my school art teacher. However, Amanda seemed very understanding and supportive so I came back the following week. I also started attending a WEA creative writing class at Hoole Community Centre which Amanda went to herself, and invited me to. Through going to the writing class, I've gained employment as a support tutor there. I respect the overall ethos of WEA towards adult education. I'm also a volunteer in Amanda's WEA art class, which evolved from a drop-in workshop. I've learned that art can be for everyone to explore and take an interest in, and I've developed my creativity and confidence.

I didn't gain what I wanted from school and college, because they didn't accommodate my particular needs, which included an eyesight difficulty. Through the WEA classes I've been involved in, I feel my learning needs have been taken care of and I've had a much more satisfactory learning experience.

Tutor Perspective: Amanda Derry

Lindsay first joined my group when it was a voluntary arts workshop, at St. Peter's Church in Chester about three years ago. When I became a WEA adult learning tutor I changed the workshop into a WEA class, with the help of

3rd Space umbrella organisation, who became partners with WEA and Andy Jurgis, my Learning Manager. The transition wasn't always an easy one, but with the help of Lindsay who became voluntary support tutor, I received strong support and encouragement, which I did need at times! I find Lindsay's enquiring attitude, contributions to the group (often through 'Show and Tells') and ability to befriend students from all backgrounds a big inspiration; and she always brings her exuberant personality to the table.

Lindsay has experienced many difficulties in her past including hip pain, which was constant until she had a replacement at the age of forty, and an eyesight disability which means she's partially sighted. She also has a motor skills impairment so she can find simple tasks difficult, which the rest of us take for granted. These obstacles haven't stopped her from gaining employment, studying, travelling and living a varied life with many interests. She has obtained employment in another WEA class (although still comes to mine) and when talking to her, she explained she feels comfortable in my class, enjoys the lessons and meeting people; and is very supportive of the class's diverse and inclusive approach:

"The Therapeutic Arts and Crafts group has enhanced my artistic skills. When I was younger I used to think that I was hopeless at art, but now I know that art is for everyone and we can all be creative. I feel relaxed when I come to the class."

Vicki Colyer, WEA

About a year ago, after suffering severe anxiety and depression following a horrific incident of domestic violence alongside personal struggles with alcohol addiction, I was introduced to Therapeutic Arts & Crafts at St Peter's Church by a friend also in recovery. At this point in my life, I had no confidence and my self-esteem and self-worth was at an all time low.

Prior to this I was a lecturer and had a successful career teaching many subjects at college and university level. However, at this time I had been unable to work, was isolating myself and rarely interacted with other people.

I started at St Peter's as a regular member of the art class and, although I had studied art at A level, I had limited technical skills as I had not kept it up. This, however, did not matter as the class included all abilities and people from all walks of life. Slowly, my confidence came back and I found it also assisted with other areas of my personal development such as applying for additional courses and looking for employment.

An opportunity then arose whereby I was asked if I would be interested in being a paid support tutor for the class that I regularly attended. As I had been out of work for two years I was still lacking in confidence somewhat. However, as this was to do a role I was familiar with and had prior experience in, I was delighted that I had been asked and I felt like this was a perfect stepping stone towards regaining the life I would like to have back. I accepted immediately and even before being interviewed realised the impact that being asked had had on my self-confidence. The support role would involve assisting certain learners with specific needs including paperwork, practical work as well as being involved with field trips when necessary, all of which I have had experience with and believe I would be able to do effectively. As a former lecturer in higher education, I understand the importance that adult learning has on the lives of individuals wanting to progress in life; and as a person who has suffered personal difficulties, I appreciate how essential finding an outlet and safe environment can be on moving forward with your life. These are two things I have found to be key within the foundation of what 3rd Space at St Peter's offers and I am truly grateful that I can now be a part of this and am able to give something back.

Tutor Perspective: Amanda Derry

I needed support from someone in my arts group who was confident with helping students in their practical artwork and paperwork and who had experience in this area. Taking students out on field trips was also a consideration. I have students with learning needs and was finding it difficult to provide the one-to-one help they required. Vicki had been in my class for a few months and mentioned she was looking for employment. When the opportunity arose I asked if she would like to be a paid support tutor and she was delighted to accept. I thought Vicki would be a good support as she had previously been an adult learning tutor, is very capable and efficient in dealing with paperwork and learners with different needs, and has a very enthusiastic approach in the class.

Vicki has experienced abuse with a former partner, and has had addiction issues. This meant she was out of the workplace for a while and her confidence had been eroded. I'm hopeful that the arts class can bring her back into employment and resurge old skills as well as learning new ones. 3rd Space, the partner organisation who run the venue the class operates under, is a well-being group aimed at helping people in need within a cultural hub of different workshops. Vicki was referred through one of the services which 3rd Space is in contact with. I feel that she can help others through her experiences, and contribute towards the group, where we support each other's personal and learning development:

"The art class at St. Peter's has reconnected me with learning a subject I loved but never took further than A level. It has reminded me of the therapeutic beauty that learning and doing art can have on your soul and well-being."

WEA

Founded in 1903, the Workers' Educational Association (WEA) is a charity and the UK's largest voluntary sector provider of adult education. In 2014/15 we delivered 9,700 part-time courses for over 70,000 students in England and Scotland with classes in almost every local authority area and our work in England was assessed in 2014 as 'Good' by Ofsted.

The WEA is committed to supporting students to develop their English and maths skills and offers a range of non-accredited and accredited courses across its nine regions in England. For many, our provision serves as a first step back into learning. It is central to our mission, vision and our approach to education and learning. Many of our English and maths students are enrolled on entry level provision, hoping to gain higher level qualifications in the future to secure employment or to further their learning. Many face a number of challenges including low self-esteem, a lack of confidence in their skills, poor pay or unemployment and challenging living conditions. We work in partnership, within communities, to reach those often hardest to reach; providing them with opportunities to develop their skills.

With the support of nearly 400 local branches, 3,000 volunteers, 2,000 part-time tutors and our active membership, the WEA provides high quality, student-centred and tutor-led education for adults from all walks of life. We bring education into the heart of communities, helping people learn whatever they want – from maths, English and skills for employment, through health and well-being courses, to cultural studies that help students broaden their horizons and community engagement programmes that encourage active citizenship.

We believe learning is for everyone and learning is for life. It helps people feel that anything is possible. It can be life-enhancing and life-changing – improving health, self-confidence and creating positive changes that ripple out from individuals to communities.

We also have a special mission to reach those who want to improve their lives and communities. Education is a beautiful and powerful tool for tackling economic and social disadvantage because it raises aspirations and helps people create their own change. We campaign for adult education and whether you want to become a student, member, volunteer, tutor or partner, you are always welcome to the WEA.

So learn the WEA way – friendly, accessible education on your doorstep. You do not need any previous knowledge or qualifications to join most of our courses, only a willingness to share with others your curiosity, ideas and experience.

Peter Miller, Argyll and Bute Council

I'm a forty-five year old male, from a manual working background, leaving school with no formal qualifications. As an adult, I was diagnosed as having dyslexia.

I came to adult education to improve my maths and my English. I was inspired by the adult literacies worker to improve my maths and English with the help of tutors. My limitations were my maths; which were stopping me becoming a firefighter. The blocks were the basic maths, but the hard maths were easy! I just wasn't getting it.

I signed up for 'WoodWord', a course which used the principles of a traditional forest school, but geared towards an adult literacy and numeracy audience. The tutors and fellow participants on the course, working as a team, helped us to solve the 'problems'.

My thought at the time was, can I do this or can I not do it? I changed my thoughts to, I can do. During the course I learned a lot, like various writing styles, and how things in the natural world change over time. My self-esteem and confidence built up over time by going to WoodWord.

I am no longer depressed and I can help my son with simple maths. Even though I am no longer a firefighter, I am able to lead a positive working life. I still have pangs of not feeling worth, but when I look back at what I have achieved, I feel that I can do what I want to do.

People starting out in adult education: it's going to be hard, but bite the bullet and go for it, because you will come out.

<u>Tutor Perspective: Brian Marden</u>
Adult Literacies Development Worker with the WoodWord Project, Argyll and Bute Council, and interviewed by Pam Staley

Taking learning to the outdoor environment has benefited a group of adults in Oban, when they joined a project which aims to develop confidence and self-esteem, along with basic skills, through hands-on experiences in a woodland setting.

The Project

The project has its roots some time ago. Janie Steel, a young woman who had been in and around the literacy service for a number of years, initially referred by Dyslexia Scotland and now trained as a Forest Schools Trainer, was looking to expand work with adults. One such project had taken place in Greater Glasgow and Clyde to promote well-being with clients, who used mental health services. Not comfortable working with this client group, Janie approached Brian Marden, Adult Literacies Development Worker in Oban, with the idea of using the Forest Schools project with an adult literacies group.

Janie and fellow Forest Schools trainer, Ross Preston of Rowan Ecology and Education Support, did not know how to integrate adult literacies skills into their programme. As quid pro quo, they both joined Brian's volunteer tutor training and Brian took on Forest Schools training. Initial discussions looked at a funding package and they applied, through Forest Schools Initiative, and were successful. WoodWord was born!

Intended Outcomes

Initial meetings took place and outcomes evolved as it went on. Standard literacy resources and forest school resources were thrown into the pot and as the project ideas took shape, the planned eight sessions soon increased to twelve; and hours per week increased from two to three, plus one mindfulness session. The group also set up the opportunity for learners to gain the John Muir Award, which added a further two hours per week. This was, however, a prerequisite of the funding package.

Another prerequisite for the funding was to have ten students. This, for Brian, was one of the biggest challenges. He spoke to every learner who had had some engagement with the literacy service over the past eighteen months, some new, some inactive and some who had been around for a while. Learners getting employment, moving away and other outside influences all contributed to this difficult challenge of engaging ten students for a twelve week course. However, ten students, all with some degree of learning difficulties and other conditions, including dyslexia, started the course. Volunteer Adult Literacy Tutor, John Nicol, also joined the group as additional support to the students.

Attributes to the project's success included having sufficient tutor to learner ratio. Everything was put over in a positive manner and there was time for everyone. If you didn't want to do something, you didn't have to, and the ethos was to encourage rather than enforce. There was also a two hour debrief to ask what worked and what didn't work, what impacted on learners, and what could be introduced to improve things. Learners themselves took control. One learner thrived in the woodland setting and encouraged other learners. One learner had been involved with Forest Schools during his time at school and had carried the impression it was for dunces. After struggling at first, he was won over and learned a lot!

Forest Schools staff chose a site and dealt with practicalities like landowner agreement. Dunollie Woods, on the north side of Oban, was the site chosen as its woodland provided the setting required, being exposed to the elements. The ethos of Forest Schools and literacies dovetail together well – that the learning experiences are learner-centred and look at learners from a wealth model. It was also important that any 'teachable moments' were built upon and scaffolding used as a learning process.

The woodland was, in itself, the main resource around which all activities were built. An example of using the outdoor setting was an evaluation exercise using a climbing rope. This was tied between trees, where the first tree was 0 and the tree at the other end of the scale, at 10. Questions were asked, e.g. "Did you enjoy yourself? Will you come back next week?" and the learner marked their answer at the relevant point on the rope.

The amount of activities the group got through was incredible and yet still leaves a lot more scope for the project to continue in the future. Some of the exercises evolved into further activities, from the imagination and dexterity used in the traditional Forest Schools exercises.

Every day started with a risk assessment, asking, 'What risks might we encounter and how can we get round them?' This became an empowering exercise for the group, e.g. If a fire was going to be lit – take the tallest person and create a no-go zone of six feet around the fire. This also included guidance on using all tools, how to carry them safely, clean and maintain them and put them away safely.

Highlights

Highlights of the project included the anecdotal discussions that took place and reactions of learners. They commented that you can leave your troubles behind: enthusiasm evidenced in running to get there or turning up in a suit after an interview. Getting the John Muir

Award was the first qualification for some. There was a general sense of empowerment and everyone felt it was a 'wonderful experience' which they would like to repeat. The wide elastic bands of the Forest School Orchestra was a favourite.

As well as all the highlights of the project, there were many other factors which characterise its success, with some evidence of long-term impact. Everyone has been on a journey and experienced the empowerment that encouragement, scaffolding, and learner centred activities, with small achievable tasks, can create.

Self-esteem, confidence and future prospects went up significantly and core skills improved overall. The project continued to flourish with each week through the relationships that built over the project. The very positive impact showed in different ways, with people getting different things from their experiences. It has proved, beyond doubt, that literacy learning lends itself well to Forest Schools and hopefully, this pilot will be the start of the on-going Woodword project for the future.

Key Lessons

The key lessons to be taken forward are 'Be prepared' and don't try too much. The pace and environment have to be adapted to suit all those there and there is much more to be gained by letting things take their time. The project does not need to be manic or full-on; time has to be given for learning to take place.

The biggest challenge was finding the number of learners required. A couple of people did not fit in with the other learners and, although they tried to separate behaviour from the person, this initially created tensions. However, things did settle down with a core group which were comfortable among themselves, which led to facilitating a positive programme.

Below I list example activities which integrated adult literacies.

Number Trail

This aims to see who can get the highest score, individually. Learners had to follow instructions printed on cards, starting by choosing a number between 1 – 10 and then carrying out addition, subtraction and multiplication. Although a prize had been offered for the highest correct answer, learners discovered the answer was always one, some making several attempts to make sure. The exercise was followed up later with a more random approach to hanging the instruction cards. Learners were told the answer was one and had then to find the cards (treasure hunt) and put them in the correct order.

Rats and Rants

Forest School activities included making research areas called quadrats. These had to be measured and marked out correctly before learners undertook identifying vegetation and estimating land cover, e.g. percentage of grass cover. The exercise was carried out three or four times and evidence sent to Scottish Natural Heritage. Brian built a literacy activity around this differentiating between 'quadrant' and 'quadrat'.

The quadrat

Using percentages using biodiversity of 100 square inset. Encouraging discussion.

How Good is our Woodland

This was a traditional Forest Schools activity. Learners, using observational and analysing skills, looked at different types of vegetation, trees, grasses, mosses, insects and mammals and had to identify how woodland supported the surrounding environment. All activities brought in literacy skills like reading and writing (recording it).

The Abbey

This was a nouns and adjectives activity. Learners began by looking at a picture of a painting and had to identify six nouns and six adjectives. This was then extended to learners taking a photo in the woodland and creating a story from it.

Tree Identification

Learners had to read tree identity tags, put in alphabetical order and tie to the appropriate tree.

Meet a tree

Learners were blindfolded and spun three times then directed to a tree. The aim was for them to try to get as much sensory information on the trees and surroundings as possible (e.g. how did you get to the tree?)

Homophones

Activity introducing homophones. A forest-related homophone found was lichen / lychen (werewolf).

Numeric activities

Numeric activities evolved during the project and included finding/ using a watch instead of a compass, telling time from the sun and measuring a tree by its shadow. The volunteer Literacy Tutor developed the 'measuring a tree by its shadow' activity and although the first attempt of using a one metre length before the tree did not work, even the mistakes were celebrated as this showed learners everyone was human.

Clearing 'Rhodies'

This led to a discussion around introduced species.

Deer foot print

Using coin to compare the size.

Tree Shaking

Learners shook trees to see what came out and to look at what the tree supported.

Repeat reading

This activity introduced using the song, This Land is Your Land, to rewrite the words. Learners were given 'Oban', 'Argyll' and 'Scotland' to rework. The chorus was also used for syllable work. This linked to the Forest Schools activity of making homemade instruments out of wood and string, then playing along to the song.

Kirsteen Hopkinson, HM Naval Base Clyde

I was asked to write a story for a digital book as an inspirational learner and my learning journey so far, as I have been nominated for an inspiration award 2015.

My Name is Kirsteen Hopkinson. All my adult life I have had self–esteem issues and confidence problems due to bullying that took place in my teenage years. This has had an adverse effect on my education and personal life as I began self-harming at the age of twelve, which continued into my adulthood.

Life changed for me when I became redundant in August 2012, due to the recession in 2008. My working hours reduced, which made life an emotional and financial struggle and comments from my career officer like, "Kirsteen, just be grateful you've got a job as you won't come to much" has stayed with me for years.

However, since starting as a cleaner at Faslane Naval base in October 2012, I have been given the opportunity to learn new skills, gain new experiences and most importantly work on my issues, as throughout my working life I have moved from one dead end job to another, with no opportunity to develop as an individual or as part of an establishment.

With the full support of my family, friends and management, in particular managers Mark Berry, Mhairi Harris and Margaret Miller, I was introduced to the e-learning centre at Faslane, where I met tutors Sam, Sharon, Kate, Katie, Jenny and Dom. The facilities at Faslane are predominately used by the forces, however, I wanted to progress and gain a career within Faslane, so as a civilian I decided to take full advantage of the service.

For me to progress into administration roles, I needed to gain a certificate in ECDL in computing with a small fee of £100 compared to university would have reached thousands. I learnt so much with ECDL, especially security. This is very informative, especially in today's society, where it's paramount to keep your computer protected and safe from everyday malware.

To my amazement, I thoroughly enjoyed my learning and my tutors would tell me, "You have the learning bug." For me it was a new sensation. My confidence grew and I began to feel better about myself and my future.

Working in Faslane enabled me to complete my ECDL, and, with family financial support, I was able to purchase my first computer. With continued support, I strived to improve my confidence. I became more enthusiastic, and hungry to learn. With so much improvement in my life, I no longer felt the need to self-harm. For my efforts I was rewarded a recommendation from RSM Royal Marines 43 commando for my hard work, and I continued to apply for admin jobs within Babcock, hoping to put my ECDL qualification, determination, and increased confidence to good use.

I wanted to give back and help promote e-learning so with the support from my tutors, I was given the opportunity to appear in the company's magazine, Clydewide, to encourage my colleagues to take on the opportunity to learn new skills and build confidence.

In November 2014 I applied for a Compliance Administrator role advertised on the company website.

The job consisted of maintaining eight thousand documents within the management system where policies, processes and procedures to facilitate the customer and management were retained.

When it came to the interview stage, with my confidence in one hand and my ECDL qualification in the other, I tried to sell myself and my skills and later was then offered the job. I started on 5th Jan 2015.

Whilst continuing to work and study I have found a new respect for maths and I have found myself enjoying division, multiplication and fractions. For example, with fractions, when simplifying the answer can be in your times tables or use the format of dividing the numerator with the denominator. I found that, if I can understand maths, I can achieve anything, so much so I have begun Functional Skills level 1 in English and with this hopefully in the future I can begin an S.V.Q. in administration and business. The sky is definitely the limit when it comes to adult learning. However, I won't 'rest on my laurels' with my new job as I will continue to learn with the e-learning centre. Look at it this way: if I can achieve all I have achieved in a few short years, what else can I achieve? What we all can learn from this is that, if I can do it, so can you. If you are a person reading this considering about adult learning, I will leave you with this thought:

"Challenge yourself with something you know you could never do, and what you'll find is that you can overcome anything."

<u>Tutor Perspective: Samantha Sherwin</u>

Kirsteen began her learning journey on 19th August 2013 where she enrolled on ECDL level 1 and level 2. She methodically worked through level 1 and achieved good results throughout her practice tests and final exams. Kirsteen completed and achieved her level 1 before her agreed programme end date. Kirsteen moved onto level 2 and again achieved good results throughout. She embraced learning and loved every second of it. As we said to Kirsteen, "you have the learning bug" and this was confirmed when, upon completion of her ECDL level 2 on 27th March 2014, she enrolled on her Functional Skills maths on 7th May 2014.

During Kirsteen's maths she struggled with a few areas but with focus and determination plus one-to-one tuition, she overcame these hurdles and happily passed her maths level 1 in January 2015.

Kirsteen has now embarked on her Functional Skills English level 1 and is working her way through the learning for this.

She is an inspiration to anyone wanting to improve their skills and who thinks they haven't the confidence to progress. Being Kirsteen's e-learning advisor is a delight for she is like a sponge and cannot get enough information!

Laura Coysh, Leasowe Early Years and Adult Learning Centre

We started English and maths for our future to be better. We started English and began with a letter. Its helped us so much in regard to education. We feel much better in the Leasowe recreation. We first found English hard and so it took time but we had a brilliant teacher who made us feel fine. When we started maths we began with a test then the teacher taught us more which made us the best. We have learnt so much every single lesson so we thank you very much for your maths and English blessing. We are sad that it has come to the end. Maths and English are our new set trend. We feel so happy with all of our work and all help that we received. We feel more confident in English and maths and what we have achieved.

Jacky, Leasowe Early Years and Adult Learning Centre

I was a literacy buddy. Then the tutor asked me did I want to do maths. I wasn't sure at first because I wasn't very good at maths but I decided to do it. I'm glad I did because I learnt so much. When I was in school I didn't really understand maths. I find the way the teacher explains things is easy to understand. I now find I am enjoying learning more about maths, which I never thought possible. I think because people have been critical of me in the past had put me off trying to achieve things but now I don't try to think about that and now just get on with things. At first I found it hard to understand maths, at first, but the more I am doing, the more I am learning and enjoying learning more about maths. I am going to come back again because I have enjoyed it and I am keen to learn more. I think the way the tutor teaches helps a lot too. It has given me a lot more confidence.

Janet Carr, Leasowe Early Years and Adult Learning Centre

The first embark into further education has been a great experience: to take me out of my comfort zone, and begin my learning journey. The support and guidance I received was excellent. I have made friends and grown in confidence.

The teaching involves group discussions, tasks, assessments, demonstrations and general feed back. Alison and Jill are both very experienced teachers, the learning is fun and set at a level to challenge and improve confidence.

In myself I feel ready to take on the challenges ahead. My hopes are to expel the myth that I am a little bit stupid. I have carried this around with me all my adult life. So, bring on the new and brilliant chapter of my educational journey.

Sharon Carr, Leasowe Early Years and Adult Learning Centre

My story begins in Feb 2015 when my sister told me about two courses she was starting: English and maths in an old school in Leasowe. So, the following week my journey began. I had enrolled on the course and began to study. I had even got my eldest daughter and her partner to join in too.

It has been a hard but enjoyable course and has helped me check my spellings and to write in double writing. I have made a few friends on my course and all of us have helped and encouraged each other.

Tracy O'Hare, Leasowe Early Years and Adult Learning Centre

As an adult learner, the experience of learning English has been positive and beneficial and I have been able to use skills in everyday life.

Most importantly, I have been able to use speaking and listening skills in everyday conversations and situations. The skill I have improved the most is listening. I have learned that listening is the most effective when reaching a conclusion in a family discussion, work debate for a resolution or making a point in a telephone conversation.

The students and tutor on my course created a positive environment and helped my confidence improve, which now helps me in everyday situations.

AV, Leasowe Early Years and Adult Learning Centre

My name is AV. I am a mother of two young children called Alex and Karis aged six and three. I'm twenty-eight years old, and wanting to improve my education. I'm currently taking an Improve Your English class, with a few other adults.

Having children inspired me to better myself and try to get a better job in the future. While I was at school, I never took my education seriously and was more interested in my friends. I left school, and worked for a number of years in jobs such as catering assistant, shop assistant, and factory work.

Now being out of work the past six years to take care of my children, I feel that I would like a better job than my previous employments. And I'd like to gain some more confidence. Now I'm on my second Improve Your English course and I feel I will get some good results to help me get to where I need to be. This will benefit me and my family greatly.

I would recommend adult classes to anyone who wants to improve themselves and sometimes there are creches available, which is a great help for mums!

H, Leasowe Early Years and Adult Learning Centre

My name is H. I am a fully qualified nursery nurse and have other qualifications such as GCSEs and various others related to a nursery nurse job role. I got made redundant after fourteen years of working for the council, over twelve months ago. This has given me some time to spend with my young daughter. My daughter now gets fifteen hours nursery funding which has allowed me to think about doing something for myself. I chose to enrol on an Improve Your English and Maths course and a computer course, to brush up on my skills and gain confidence.

I would have done courses sooner but I have found it hard to find courses that fit in with my daughter's nursery hours. I have, however, overcome this by slightly adjusting nursery hours and finding out if courses running have creche facilities. I hope these courses will give me the confidence to use the skills to get back into work and help when the time comes with my daughter's homework.

I would encourage any adult wanting to learn on these courses as they're a good confidence boost and like me you might do better than what you thought!

Lynda Blair, West Kirby library

I really enjoyed school but was particularly weak at maths due to lots of disruption in our maths class. I always enjoy learning. I have found it difficult when I have been at work doing end of day banking – my stress levels shoot up as I am not confident when checking large figures.

I feel it definitely knocks my confidence on so many levels. I would like to feel I could organise the family household budget, and always ask my husband to double check my work.

I am really desperate to improve and feel it will definitely add to my confidence.

Joey Cosgrove, Bebington library

I wanted to get back to education anyway. I want to get better at maths. I need to improve to help me get a job. My learning journey started with a referral from my Job Centre Plus adviser. I was assessed and put into English and maths classes at Bebington Library. My journey is ongoing, my basic skills have improved and my self-confidence is so much higher.

Ml, Bebington library

2012 Made a decision to go to maths class! Big decision as I hated maths at school and was no good at it!

2013 Been at maths for a year now. Learning maths concepts which I can actually understand. Have some concepts of the dreaded fractions!

2014 Only meant to stay at maths for a year and here I am again! I am enjoying classes and have learnt a lot. Feeling more confident and that I have achieved a lot. I have actually sat some test papers.

2015 Year three and I'm still here! Feel as if I have come a long way and sat many tests now. Even if I have failed, I still have a better knowledge of maths concepts. Able to help my children with her homework and able to do everyday things, i.e. measurement, percentages, fractions, conversion ratios. Very stimulating for me and learning.

Hope to continue my classes and get some qualifications in maths. Have enjoyed learning and being back at 'school' – something I did not think I would when I started in 2012.

Emma Smith, Ganney's Meadow Nursery School

I started at school. At first I was good at maths and in top sets but then I began to fall behind. I never liked school as I'm not much of a people person. I left school at the age of fifteen, as I wanted to be a dental nurse. After a little while I left and started work in Marks and Spencer. I worked there for six years due to having my little boy Damon. Then came Ellie. Then my little flower Poppy. Before I knew it all three kids were in school and bringing homework home. I found myself unable to help them as I didn't understand the work.

All three of my children are very bright. My youngest, Poppy, has autism and is a whizz with numbers so she gets extra homework. Now my three children are older and now I want to make them proud of their mummy. I want to be able to help them with their homework. I would love one day to become a teaching assistant (TA) but maybe for special needs as I find people don't understand how their minds work and I do with having my little flower. So, here I am today starting right from the starting point in maths. I don't find maths easy but I'm keen to learn as I want to make something of myself and better my family's life. This time I'm ready for the challenges ahead and I'm not giving up until I've reached my goals. I feel lucky with this maths course as I like the group and the teacher seems to understand me as a person which is nice. It makes coming each week easier.

Rachel Cary, Ganney's Meadow Nursery School

When I was in school, my teachers were often (VERY often)... side tracked with other pupils in my class because they were misbehaving, making jokes, throwing things, using their phones, etc. Therefore not much work ever got done. For that, I was unable to learn anything but the basics in some subjects. When exams came, I didn't get the grades I needed to get on to the college course I was hoping for.

Luckily, I still got into college, just on a lower grade course. In my final year of college I discovered that I was pregnant and had to leave the course due to health risks of losing the baby (working with animals). Whilst pregnant and in the first year after having my baby boy, I was unable/not allowed to do anything with my life because my son's dad demanded me to stay home and be a housewife. After splitting up with him and moving back home to the Birkenhead area, I was able to get my life back on track and build up my confidence again. Therefore, I thought to join courses to help me build up knowledge to progress onto/into other colleges, to get a decent job.

Sam Deer, Ganney's Meadow Nursery School

1 Left school, wasn't interested in education.

2 Started Liverpool Community College doing travel and tourism. Didn't like it.

3 Started Wirral Met doing health and social, had personal problems, so left.

4 Went back a few weeks later and completed it.

5 Fell pregnant, and then decided I wanted to be a midwife.

6 Started maths and English at Ganney's Meadow to better myself.

7 Once I finish here, go to Wirral Met and do a pre access course and hopefully uni in a few years to better my and my son's future with a good job.

Anne Ward, Ganney's Meadow Nursery School

I never done well in school as I was always distracted and lost interest and I was nervous about my work.

I have joined this maths group as I want a qualification or a GCSE result to help me find a job and so that I don't worry about money and also to show my family that I can achieve this by being confident and trying my best at all things in maths. I need more practice with most things but will keep trying different things to help me. If I do not succeed this time I will keep at it on another course. But hopefully I will do well.

I have enjoyed this maths course as everybody is lovely and friendly and the teacher Jill explains things clearly so that you can understand what you are meant to be doing and you feel relaxed and don't have to rush your work.

Jordan Pearson, St James Centre

We eagerly feed of life's fruit, knowledge, hoping to endlessly develop ourselves to a better understanding of our existence. We do this through education and learning. It's one thing that connects nearly every single human being. In a combined worldwide effort to understand why we are here and do we ultimately have a purpose, and that question is what drives and what inspires people to reach that bit further. To read another book, take another course, to move that little bit closer to a complete understanding of why we exist. And how we can better ourselves and this can only be done in education.

Liam Holman, Wirral Lifelong and Family Learning Service

1 Hello I am Liam. I am come here to learn new skills to do better in life.

2 I just went to school but I would like to learn more.

3 I found I was moving around a lot and I was with bad people. Hanging around with them didn't help my learning.

4 People have helped me to move and make new friends. I am now in a happier place.

5 The English class I am now attending will help me learn new skills and it will help me looking for a new job.

6 I would say good luck to new learners and all the best with learning and stay happy.

Ian, Wirral Lifelong and Family Learning Service

My name is Ian and I live in Wallasey. I did A levels in school and went to university but it didn't pan out.

I did some retail course and from that did a City and Guilds exam in English and maths. I noticed my limitations were in punctuation and grammar and I sought to overcome these failings. My shortcomings in punctuation held me back in writing a CV properly so I sought to overcome these shortcomings by writing stories by myself and doing role playing on role playing boards, where I was helped by some people on these boards. I hope that adult education will help me further improve these skills and help me get a job.

For those that are not sure about going into adult education, I say just give it a chance. You can only improve yourself and they cater to various skill levels so you won't be left out. You haven't got anything to lose by giving it a shot!

Kumi Takeoka, TAFE Northern Sydney Institute

I am Kumi Takeoka and I was born in Japan. I arrived in Australia in 2011. I have studied English at TAFE since I came here. I need to improve my English to live in Australia, because I need to communicate with my daughter's teacher and her friends' parents. English is necessary for me to live in Australia. Also, I want to work as a carer in Aged Care which is my career in Japan, so for that I studied Certificate III in Aged Care last year. The course was very difficult for me, but I could learn several things and I made some friends who have the same dream as me. I studied medical knowledge which is very useful when I go to the GP. I think studying as an adult is hard, but it is good for your life. I don't think I will learn if I stay in Japan. I am glad that I have the opportunity to study here.

James Zhang, TAFE Northern Sydney Institute

My name is James Zhang. I was born in Heibei, China. I came to Australia in November 2010. When I arrived in Australia, I found it was hard for me to find a job, because my English was not good, so I began to learn English at TAFE as an adult student. After two years of studying, my English is now much better than before. Meanwhile, I have learned many skills in English study, and all these skills can also be applied to many other fields of my life. What is more, I have learned a lot about Australian history, culture and its national features. It is really good for me to get merged into the society soon. I have also made some new friends at TAFE. I would like to say to people who are thinking about study, that being an adult student has a lot of benefits. It is not only a way to improve your English, but you can get self-improvement in many aspects, and you can enrich your life as well.

Xuemei Fu, TAFE Northern Sydney Institute

My name is Xuemei, and I was born in Hubei, China. I have lived in Australia since August 2013. It was quite difficult for me to find a similar Human Resources position in Australia, because my English writing skills are really poor. I missed an opportunity to work with a Hong Kongese international trade company two years ago, because the position needs to use English via emails between the clients and suppliers every day. So, I have to choose to study as an adult, because I really want to improve my reading and writing skills.

After one term of study, I have conquered the fear of writing in English, and my writing has much improved. I would like to suggest to other adults who want to improve their life and technical abilities to just go back to study. Studying as an adult, not only can you learn skills you need, but also open your mind and get some new ideas for your life. Studying as an adult also made me many new friends as well.

Mirim Kim, TAFE Northern Sydney Institute

My name is Mirim Kim, and I was born in Incheon in Korea. I have been in Australia since 2015.

The main reason that I have studied as an adult student is that I want to work as a psychotherapist in organisations like Unicef, and English is basic for it. Also, I want to study in Australia and overseas. In addition, studying as an adult has improved my life a lot because I have made friends from other countries, and I have a chance to get a better job. Moreover, it makes overseas trips easy since many countries use and understand English.

I think that studying as an adult is a good chance as well as a challenge for self-development. I know it is very difficult for adults to learn something new like language, but learning new things is a worthwhile activity. If they look back later, I'm sure that they will not regret it.

Eun Kyung Choe, TAFE Northern Sydney Institute

My name is Eun Kyung and I was born in South Korea. I have been living in Australia since 2011. In this year, I'm studying as an adult student, because I would like to break my language barrier, and then fulfil my goal. It is an effective way to improve my life. For example, it gives me confidence when I communicate with others. Also, I can participate in my son's school events as a volunteer parent. It is a great change in my life. Studying as an adult has a lot of difficulties. However, it can provide good chances to you. You can change your life worthily through this. Therefore, I recommend studying to you. Don't hesitate.

Maria Sergeeva, TAFE Northern Sydney Institute

My name is Maria Sergeeva. I was born in Moscow, Russia. I have been living in Australia since 2014.

I chose to study English immediately when I came to Australia because I wanted to integrate in Australian social life. Knowledge of English is a necessity to stay in an English-speaking country. Study as an adult is improving my life. This allows me to improve my self-development, modify my English skills, as well as helping me communicate with people, and enlarging my circle of friends. Moreover, study as an adult helps me feel confident and proud of myself. Furthermore, it helps me to find a job and take more life benefits.

I would say to other adults who are thinking about study that it is a good experience, which improves your life and provides more opportunities.

It is never too late to learn. The main thing is to start and then have fun.

Lizzie Addison, Learn Devon

I started my first course at Bideford Arts Centre four years ago. I am visually impaired and I decided to do some courses to help me become more independent. I believed that I could do more than what I had learnt at school. I went to a college for visually impaired pupils. I did not do any English, maths or ICT at school. Things I did at school were learning to clean, learning to help in the nursery and to look after the flowers and plants. We used to cook our own lunches with some help.

I learnt about adult learning when I came to The Hub in the same building where they ran the courses. I registered for my first course which was English and maths and learnt so much that I decided to keep on learning.

I also believed that doing more courses would help me to communicate easier and understand more things better. I did some art courses and continued my English and maths. I started using the computer and soon my ICT skills got better. I have given some PowerPoint presentations in class which made me feel good and happy. The art courses helped me to do creative things. I realised that being visually impaired doesn't have to stop you from making beautiful things. When I started to use a computer I learnt to type with my special keyboard and that helped me to spell some words myself. I soon learnt to make PowerPoint presentations and do research on Google.

I have now started working in a charity shop. Without the maths skills I learnt I would not be able to work with money and on a till. I also deal with customers. I got the confidence to work with people by being part of adult learning.

My life has changed a lot since I enrolled onto my first course.

I have met lots of different people and realised that I am good at working in a team. I participated in art exhibitions and I welcomed the public at the door and showed them to the drinks counter. I would never have dreamt of doing so before I started the courses.

My money skills have got better since doing maths and I now have the confidence to pay for things myself when I get the chance.

I think doing the courses has changed me as a person. I feel very proud of myself for what I have achieved. I have got loads of certificates for my hard work and I feel confident that the future will bring more happy things for me.

Patrick Sellick, Learn Devon

Before I started learning, I was miserable and not myself. I didn't get out much. I had a bad accident when I was young, which means I can't use my left arm properly, and I have other health problems. I started the courses because I wanted to get more experience and learn new things.

For eight years I have been going to college to do different courses, including Preparing to Work with Children and Young People, English and maths. I also did a course about Hate and Mate Crime and went on to give talks about it. I have gained a lot of certificates and experience. I passed my Diploma in English and maths* which made me very proud.

A few years ago I won an Adult Learner's Award** (now Festival of Learning) and went to a ceremony in Exeter.

Learning has changed my life. I have got more patience now to do things, and with other people I am more confident and outgoing and friendly. I am socialising more and have met a lot of people this year.

I am looking after myself better and have had the courage to get my hearing and eyesight tested. I try to help other people stay healthy, get help and not get into trouble.

My writing and reading is good. I only need a little help with some spellings now.

I am extremely independent. I have found out that I can do more things by myself. I have a lot of respect for myself and I am a caring, kind man. I am a volunteer working with children at my church, and I love and respect the children I work with. I am a good team player and work well with others.

I have recently started to enjoy cooking, mostly baking, and in the New Year I will be learning more about healthy eating and getting fitter.

Now I'm able to leave some of the bad stuff in my life behind and look forward to the future.

*OCR Life and Living Skills (entry level 2) **Certificate of Achievement (South West)

Star Spencer, Learn Devon

I was born prematurely on July the 25th 1984 after a three day labour.

I could not walk until I was three years old. Dad told me the funny story of how he put some sweets on the table and I got up and walked to get them. He was amazed. It was a big achievement overcoming that.

By the time I was in my twenties I was living independently, with a carer to help. I did courses with the Prince's Trust in 2009 and when that finished I didn't want to just do nothing with my life, I wanted more.

I came to Devon Adult and Community Learning (now known as Learn Devon) at the Bideford Arts Centre six years ago. I felt very down about the way I looked at the time. I started my learning here with Everyday Maths and English and other courses such as Work Matters, Drama Matters and Movie Making.

With the support of our tutor we got our fundraising team ('The FUNdraisers') together. We have done a number of charity events and raised money for Shelter Box, Kira Farm in Uganda and Toilet Twinning. The one I enjoyed the most was my very first event with the team, Winter Wonderland dance.

Adult learning has made me think that I can achieve more in life and it has added to my quality of life. I have met different people on the way with different hobbies, dreams and hopes for their future too.

Through my hard work I received an Adult Learners Award (now Festival of Learning) in 2012* with a ceremony at a very posh hotel in Weston Super Mare. I even got to meet the eighties icon Cheryl Baker from Bucks Fizz. Never in my life would I have expected to meet a celebrity. It was the highlight of my year and while receiving my award I had three cuddles from the great lady herself.

I like to think that we have made friendships for life here in the groups at Bideford Learn Devon, as they do really make you feel very welcome. Being here is like a support group and a self-made family too.

Being at Learn Devon and having new skills has made me not shy away from things and not freeze. It has made me feel I can achieve anything I put my mind to. It has also given me the skills to have the confidence to get a job. As a result of these courses I also believe that I would meet a partner at some time in my life and build our lives together.

*Certificate of Achievement (South West)

Elizabeth Napangardi Lechleitner

Standing on my Own Two Feet

I was born and raised in Yuendumu, which is in Warlpiri country in the Tanami Desert. My mother is Western Arrente and my father is Warlpiri/Amatjerre. I went to school in Alice Springs and then lived on an out-station between Papunya and Hass Bluff. My mum passed away when I was a young girl and I got a lot of strength from my brother Kenny Japangardi.

A difficult situation was having my first child and being a mother when I was so young. Why was it difficult? Not knowing what you are in hospital for. It was scary but the nurse was a good help and explained everything. What made me feel better was that I had a lot of help from my sister, talking to the nurses and other family members like my young cousin. My cousin was in the same age group as me and had kids before me and talked about what she went through.

I had two children by the time I was twenty-two years of age and living in Warlpiri camp, which is one of the town camps in Alice Springs. Being a young mother is a big commitment and also a big responsibility.

At that time I was going out a lot, partying and stuff like that. I was going through a rough time and was separated from my partner. My brother, Kenny

Japangardi, sat me down and asked what I wanted to do with my life. I thought about it and told him I always wanted to be a police officer.

One winter night I put the kids to bed and was looking at them while they were asleep. I thought to myself, I could walk out tomorrow, go shopping in town and get hit by a car and my kids would have nothing. I am on a Centrelink benefit and there wouldn't be anything for my kids to fall back on if I wasn't there. My family was there but it is different without a mother – I learnt that when I was young and lost mine. I was still thinking about joining the police and I did that like the next day and started my police training. I think it is having my kids that has given me resilience because I never want them to feel like they are not looked after. It has been difficult but when I am in a stressed situation, I breathe deeply, stay calm and talk in a quiet tone of voice.

What I would say to young people? Go to school and get a job and maybe travel the world before you settle down and meet other people.

Tutor Perspective: Ros Bauer

Elizabeth Napangardi Lechleitner is an Indigenous woman from central Australia. Her mother is Western Arrente and her father is Warlpiri/Amatjerre. Luritja, Warlpiri and Amatjerre are Lizzie Napangardi's thee first languages and English is her fourth language. She currently works in Yuendumu supporting families to engage with school; and studies through the Batchelor Institute in Yuendumu, in the Northern Territory. Lizzie Napangardi is a hard working woman and has consistently held jobs in the community that support families in different ways. Lizzie's language skills enable her to code switch seamlessly and as such is a highly valuable and sought after team member. She cares for her immediate and extended family, is adored by her grandchildren and loves nothing more than 'going bush' to get away from it all.

Debbie Weldon, MTC Maroubra

Being a single mother, I became isolated from the world and the changes that were happening. With computers becoming prevalent, I decided to learn about them. I chose a course Women out of Work designed for my age. It was very challenging, as I did not own a computer, and couldn't even turn one on. I was the odd one out in the class for many reasons.

Suffering from panic attacks and anxiety, I found it hard to even get through the induction. I struggled with leaving the house, and catching a train to get to college. Finding classrooms was the biggest challenge. In class, my lack of finances was obvious in my dress, at lunch time and in interaction with other class members. My teachers were helpful and patient. Frustrated, stressed and down-hearted, I persisted.

Knowing this would change my world; giving up was not an option. With the routine of classes, I found it easier to find my way around and even a reason to get out of bed. One of the other ladies in the class gave me her old computer, so I could practise. I passed the assessments in class and now with my new skills the world is open to me.

With my new found confidence, I attended the end-of-course party and group photo. At fifty years of age, I booked an aeroplane and hotel and went on my first holiday. I also can write resumes and cover letters, which has helped me gain employment. I bought a computer and now use it to store photos and videos, which I use to make CDs for my family. I also make birthday cards and party invitations for my grandchildren, who are very impressed with Nana's skills.

As my family live in remote areas, I can plan my transport and email my schedule so I can visit them without them worrying about my journey. Again this is something my grandchildren enjoy. I have found I enjoy learning and have the confidence to enrol and complete other courses.

Thank you.

Victor Isla, MTC Maroubra

Since my arrival in Australia in July 1980, I was determined to work hard to save a deposit to buy a home for my family. We were tired of renting and having to move from one property to another. During this time, I also studied screen printing at the Sydney Technical College (Now known as TAFE) to improve my skills and find a better job. After we finally bought our first home, my wife worked hard as a stay-at-home mother to look after our young daughters. I decided to find a second job to help speed up our mortgage payments. I worked twelve hours per day Monday to Friday, and five hours part-time on Saturday. After fifteen years of hard work and long hours, I finally saved enough to repay the bank in full. The day my wife and I finalised our mortgage, we felt relieved that our dream of owning our home had come true. These days, we are able to live in our home without the burden of any mortgage or rent payments.

David Lane, MTC Maroubra

To deal with resilience. Facing the stress and trauma that life throws up at me. Not having any work for two years is a stressful time for me, having to look for work and not having the confidence in finding the right one that will suit me. Also, having to deal with the financial situation.

Trying to budget can be difficult. Working out how much food to buy for the week at a cheap price, and to make it last without throwing the food away. To be careful what to buy and when to buy it. Being a father of a child whom I do not see is also a stressful time in my life. The worry of how he is coping or doing in his life makes me feel like I failed as a father or dad. To find ways to deal with these situations is not easy. I find that I need to take care of myself and do not let the problem get to me.

Living in the city of Sydney can be stressful sometimes with the noise. Some people's attitudes can also be annoying. The trouble I get myself into is ridiculous. The fines and court appearances can sometimes be a headache. It is like I have to lock myself in my room and not talk to anyone, in case I get into trouble. That is the feeling I get sometimes. It is like living in an outside prison sometimes. And then you get all this advice on how to run your own life, like being told what to eat and how to eat it. Then having to deal with these things from day to day can test your stress levels. So, to be more positive about being down and feeling sorry for myself, I switch my mind towards the things that I like to do.: maybe go for a swim or some sort of exercise, ride a bike, go for a walk.

I also like my sports, so I will read about the horse races or football to see who is winning. I find this to be enjoyable and passes time quickly. I also socialize with the room-mates at home where I live, maybe give someone a hand with a hobby that they may be working with. For example, cleaning my friend's boat or car. And if that's not happening, I will do some cleaning, tidy up my room or kitchen just to keep busy and get my mind off those negative thoughts that I may be having. And I will also do some cooking or prepare a good meal.

Never give up... when things are tough. Persevere and build resilience.

Anon, MTC Maroubra

This is a story about a single mother. Her name is Hazel. Hazel had a five year old daughter named Daisy. Hazel had been in a ten year relationship with Daisy's father. Although Daisy's father was not physically abusive, he was verbally abusive and controlling.

When Daisy was four years old she asked her Mummy if they could leave and find a new Daddy. Within days Hazel packed the two of them up and moved in with Daisy's grandmother in Sydney.

Hazel was not very confident and found it difficult looking for a unit of their own. Hazel was struggling with being a single parent. After one and a half years Hazel found the right home for herself and Daisy. Daisy started school for the first time and settled into her new life with her mummy.

When Daisy was six years old, Hazel met a man at a friend's barbeque, who was also a single father himself. Daisy liked him very much. Although this new man, who we will call Peter, never moved in with Daisy and her mum, he was around a lot.

After one year, Hazel discovered she was pregnant with Peter's baby. Both Daisy and Hazel were very happy to be having a new baby in the family. Although Daisy liked Peter, he sometimes scared her when he would yell at her Mummy and break things.

After Daisy's sister was born, life for Daisy and Hazel got progressively more violent and disruptive. Hazel would break up with Peter and try to get on with life with two young daughters. But Peter would always be trying to come over or call, pleading to see Hazel and the girls. Hazel's self-esteem and confidence was at an all-time low.

Peter would beg and promise that the violence would stop and that he would change for the children and Hazel. But after a couple of weeks, Peter would get angry, and the violence and chaos would start all over again.

The Department of Community Services became involved. They removed the girls from Hazel's care, saying Hazel was too sympathetic to Peter and that the children's lives were at risk. Hazel was suffering from depression and anxiety. She admitted herself into a rehabilitation program for three months.

When Hazel finally came home, she continued to see a psychologist and got legal aid, a wonderful lawyer, and took the department to court to try and get her children returned. Daisy eventually went to live with her father full time. After years of fighting with the court system, Hazel slowly started making progress, getting Daisy's little sister returned.

Throughout all these years and struggles, Hazel has learnt that she is stronger and more resilient than she ever realised or imagined. Now Hazel knows that no matter what people say or do to try and pull her down or say she will never make it, she has the strength and ability within to know better and not give up.

Hazel now gets up every morning with a new sense of purpose and confidence. Hazel has learned that she is very resilient, strong and committed when she needs to be. This whole experience has made Hazel the mother and woman she is today.

Anon, MTC Maroubra

This is a story of abuse and resilience through the eyes of a ten year old. It all started many years ago. I had just turned ten and my dad was getting out of jail. All I ever wanted was a dad. When he got out, I moved in with him, even though my mother did not want me to go. But I went anyway, and it broke her heart.

So, the first few months were ok. Then the sexual, physical, and mental abuse started. I did not know who to turn to. I thought I was the only one he was touching and doing this stuff to, but little did I know he was doing it to my cousin when she stayed over. I never realised why he always told me to ask if my cousin was allowed to stay over. I thought it was so I would have someone to play with. My cousin was nine. The abuse carried on till I was fifteen, and my dad went back to jail for drug dealing. He also had me dealing heroin for him. He would make me carry it so if the police pulled us over, there was a better chance the police would not search me. I was his slave.

Three years ago, my cousin came forward and brought charges against my dad. Then four more girls came forward. I was not one of them, as I was scared, and still am. My dad got ten years in jail. It is only now that I have started to move on, and put it all behind me. I spent ten years of my life on ice and heroin, in and out of jail, and lost my two children. I am lucky my mum took my kids. I have been out of jail now for one year and am drug free.

I am on the methadone program but I am ok with that. I am getting the help I need. I go to counselling once a week. I have a support worker that I can ring at any time if I feel the need. I am also doing a computer course. I see my kids every day. I am really sorry for the life I gave my kids up till now - worrying more about where my next hit was coming from, rather than looking after them. I was self-medicating, trying to suppress the shame of what happened to me when I was a child. I am starting to trust people again. I feel like I have come so far in such a short time.

Dancy O'Hara, MTC Maroubra

The death of an ogre

Once upon a time, there was a King and Queen who lived in Cittia. Cittia was a very busy place. Lots of people lived there. It was easy to get lost in the crowd.

The King and Queen had a Princess girl and a Prince boy. Life was nice, but the King had a deep dark secret, and he didn't know how to deal with it. The darkness started to eat his soul like a spiteful ogre. He began to loathe his beautiful family, and slowly after time he tortured the love out of his family.

The Prince boy was sad, for the King and Queen outlawed playing and singing. The Prince boy did not like this new rule, as he could not stop playing and singing. His punishment was to be locked away in a tower with no doors, guarded by a dragon.

The Queen was torn by her love for the King and her children. She couldn't stop crying, and flooded the kingdom with all her tears. The kingdom was drowning, so she was banished to a land far away. The land was hot and horrible, where her tears could do no harm.

The Princess girl also loved the King but no matter how hard she tried, she could not make the King see what he had done to his family. The Princess girl had a deep aching inside her heart. Nothing could undo the broken heart which heavily burdened her. She travelled to new lands, trying to find an elixir to mend her heart.

Many years had passed, and the Queen had made a new life in the barren land. She was happy now. The Queen had many animal friends.

The Prince boy could nearly escape the tower – the dragon was very old and very close to death. All he had to do was bide his time, and the dragon would perish.

The Princess girl tried to keep the kingdom together, but to no avail. The King continued with his hateful ways. The King died, choking on a grape, and his hateful legacy died with him.

The Princess girl eventually found the elixir, but not the way she had imagined. She gave birth to a beautiful golden boy, and she promised she would never pass on the things she was taught. She would teach her son to love, and be loved in return.

The End

Monique Harris, MTC Maroubra

Hope

Day to day: living from day to day, coping with life's chores can be rewarding, yet very stressful for anyone.

Falling sick: then you fall sick. At first, it's pretty cool. You lie in bed all day, no work, no cleaning, and no worrying about anything. Just relax, sleep and be waited on.

Pain: then the pain sets in. Wow! Cleaning and working isn't looking too bad now. The day to day stresses of life were pretty simple compared to this pain.

Depressed: feeling useless in a bed day after day, week after week, can make you go a little crazy, and feel a bit depressed.

Finding Hope: taking yourself out of a dark place isn't easy, but with faith, hope and will power, anything is possible.

Should Do: dreaming

Reality: awake

Victory: you did it!

Trust in yourself: but never give up. Trust in yourself, have a little faith and hope, and you will overcome anything.

Paul Pisani, MTC Maroubra

I was born in Australia in 1965. My father was Maltese, but was born in Port Said, Egypt and was a British subject. His family originally came from Malta, but moved to Egypt to work for the Suez Canal Company in 1914 as shipbuilders. They built coal barges and tugs out of both wood and steel.

My mother was Italian, and was born in Sicily. Her family came from the Seven Volcanic Islands near Sicily, which were ancient. They traded in salt with the Spanish Empire.

When I was five years old, I went to kindergarten at St. Andrew's School, Malabar. In 1975, when I was ten years old, I started at Marist Brothers School, Daceyville, where I was placed in the ESL (English as a Second Language) system. It was thought wrongly that I would not be able to speak, read and write English, because I came from an ethnic Italian background that at that time were hostile to foreign people they assumed had fascist leanings.

The people who ran the schools were English and had a bad experience of fascism. The Italians had surrendered to the English in 1943 in North Africa. They were sent to internment camps for the duration of the war, as punishment. In Australia, the Italians were rounded up and taken to internment camps in South Australia where they stayed from 1940 until after the war ended in 1946. When they came out, the Australian people did not trust them with their looks, strange clothes and language. The solution was to set up an education system that separated the Italians from the Anglo-Saxon white children.

This system was called ESL, where other children and I were taught English. We were taught how to read, write and spell, and were told about the English way of life and the British Empire. We had to use spelling cards, and would have to write out the same letter in an exercise book. We were not allowed to speak our mother tongue or talk about other countries or where our parents came from. In later years, it became difficult for me to talk to my parents in Italian. This nonsense came to an end when the education department changed policy. I went back into a normal classroom, but I was always at the back and left behind. The teacher did not want to teach maths and was not interested in me. When the government stopped the ESL experiment, the school gave up on me and themselves. The school shut down and is now the Catholic Education Office.

Nobody wants to talk about ESL any more, and many retired teachers still defend this wrong system. They claim it was right and I am wrong, that they were trying to teach me English, and make me forget about my Italian background.

Belle Hona, MTC Maroubra

My story about resilience simply means for me to bounce back, even higher and stronger after a set back. It becomes a character strength when we form a habit of bouncing back. I know I will bounce back from my situation and I refuse to feel sorry for myself. There are many things in my life I like to be thankful for. Changing our attitude is more difficult than anything else, so yes, this is a challenge.

Charan Dass, OAE

I am Mr Charan. I am a new migrant to Australia. Basically being Indian I spent most of my life time in the defence services. Now after retirement I came here to live with my children and grandchildren. I feel proud to be an Australian beginning my next generation, enjoying helping my grandchildren and leading an active cheerful life with their company.

When I landed here in Australia, I had difficulty in communicating with the local people around me. It was because of my poor English. I was intending to integrate into the Australian society and work culture. Therefore it was very necessary for me to enhance my English knowledge, with the result I had to find a suitable institute and I was lucky enough to get enrolled in the Olympic Adult Education (OAE) course where mature and senior people like me can learn and upgrade skills.

As I started my course in this institution I felt very happy because the syllabus here taught is to the perfect standard which is helping me a lot in my learning English. The most influencing thing here is that the course is more practically oriented. The teaching staff here is splendid and pleasing. We experienced problems with listening, and the teacher advised me to listen to ABC television channel news, and it was very helpful too. After completing the first term of our course, we were able to speak and listen to our classmates in English. We have improved a lot and got confidence to face an interview or go to the GP and explain our problems, or interact with official staff.

Doing the English course helped a lot with my English skills. I can communicate with my neighbours and go shopping on my own. I could go to any office and talk to the staff and get any help I needed. Certainly the quality of life has improved. As my communication skills have improved a lot, my family members and friends feel very proud of me. I can now move around independently, talk to people and share my ideas with friends in the community.

The moment I complete my course I will be able to express myself and my experiences during the studies, and exhibit the speaking and listening standards I have attained here. Thereby I will be a good influence on the people who are in search of a good education which is more practically oriented. My acquired English knowledge will itself reflect the standards of Olympic Adult Education (OAE) in society.

Issak Ibrahim, OAE

I am a student in OAE. My background is that I come from Somalia. I came to Australia in 2001. I had a lot of study in my country – typing, Italian, Arabic and a little English. I finished high school, I started university and studied agriculture with Italian language for two years, and then civil war started in 1996.

I started to work at ICRC (International Committee of the Red Cross) as a medical team member. I worked for one year. Then the war got worse. After, I fled to Kenya to a camp for four years. Then I came to Australia with my two children and my husband. First I started level one English, level two, and then I started Certificate III Childcare Service and Diploma. Now I study level three and advanced computers.

I need a childcare qualification to get a job. A job is very important for me so I can support my family. I have a small problem with English because it's not my first language. I have a lot of homework to do at home so I have to do it when my children are asleep.

My self helps me to decide to keep studying. Some friends told me about Olympic and then I started coming. Before, I didn't know about this English course, even though I studied to get my driver licence.

Now I'm living with my husband and my children and I study English. I am looking after my children and still have to improve my English language but my life is better than before. I can write a little more now and I never give up my goals. Since I have studied I can talk with people more and I feel more comfortable because English is very important for society. I don't want to create extra work for myself. Now I have got my licence and understand conversation.

I love to talk in my community about how to improve my English. I help my children with homework and I talk to my children in English and with my friends and my colleagues. I would tell my friends to come to OAE. I push and say, "Come and join us at Olympic to learn," because I got confidence. I now understand the different multi-cultures. Before, I was shy to talk to other people because I was not confident in English.

Gabriela Grisolia, OAE

I am Gabriela Grisolia. I come from Venezuela. I speak Spanish. I was studying marketing in 2004. I worked at a truck company for about nine years. I have been in Australia for five years. I started studying English from the very beginning. Now I can speak Spanish and a little English. I decided to come back to study English because I would like to feel confident, and improve my speaking and writing in English. In the future, I am looking for a job in an office for example.

My principal inspiration was and is my kids, my self, to have a good quality of life and lots of opportunities. My options are short courses, but I don't have the time and money for continuing my degrees.

When I began to study English in Australia, I was shy and afraid because I didn't speak English. I didn't know about many things and I felt scared. I missed my family and friends in my country. I was worried about my new life and if it was the right option to move to Australia or not. When I arrived in Australia my son started childcare. When I left and picked up my son, I couldn't understand what the staff told me about my son. I felt horrible and disappointed.

Now I am studying English at Olympic Adult Education (OAE). I feel happy and I want to learn more about English and different subjects. I think learning at an adult education centre will improve my speaking and writing. When I finish my courses I can feel confident about my skills. I can help my kids at school. I could update my skills and I can do whatever I like in the future. I always said to my son, "You can do anything, whatever you like when you practice and practice. Don't worry."

I talk to my friends and tell them you need to try to speak in English as much as possible and read and listen to the radio.

Bawk Nang Lahtaw, OAE

My name is Bawk Nang Lahtaw. I came from Myanmar. I have been in Australia over three years. I came from a refugee background. I lived in Malaysia for three years. I got a UNHCR (United Nations High Commissioner for Refugees) card in 2009. After three years, I arrived in Australia. I have been studying at an adult education college at Olympic Village. Before I started I could write and talk English. I have built my English skills. My writing skills and listening skills have improved now. I have always inspired myself to study my English. I really need to talk to people. No-one can stop me.

I studied English at AMES Flagstaff in 2012. I have done Certificate III in Commercial Cookery Kitchen in 2015 in Australia. I have been working at Isabella Pizza shop since 2015. I have learnt how to cook dishes and how to make sauces. I loved to cook foods.

I have many challenges. My colleagues helped me to speak and learn how to pronounce words. Sometimes, I don't know what to call a thing, and how to pronounce it, but my friends are helping me at work.

I have been studying English at level 2 and level 3 now. I have a job. I'm looking after my daughter and taking care of her. When I go to school, I put her in childcare.

My speaking, listening, writing, grammar and pronunciation have all improved at Olympic Adult Education, and contributed to improving my quality of life. I can talk more and understand more now. My family have helped my English too. My friends and my community have better speaking skills than me. They have been pushing me to speak English too. I can read stories to my daughter. I can sing to her now. I take her to the library for children's activities.

I will just continue studying English classes now. When I first started to study English, I did not have any good writing skills, but now I have some idea of it. I will improve my English skills. I will learn at the adult education centre until I'm very good at English.

Faiza Abdullahi, OAE

I'm a Somali woman. I come from Somalia and I'm a student. I am studying ESL because I would like to improve my English skills and go to university. First of all my needs inspired me. That was my biggest motivation. Secondly I have had a lot of support from different organisations and people, for example my family, friends, my teachers, government support and my class mates.

I had a lot of interruption, e.g. health issues, going overseas, having a family with a busy life and many other things. I have been very determined to continue. Also I have had a lot of support from different people like family and friends. Actually I'm at Olympic Adult Education, in the middle of my study. I think I can study and reach my goal. Now, I feel more confident to go to many places I need and do many things I wasn't able to do before, for example driving and speaking English.

I feel more comfortable to help my family, friends and colleagues, and I also communicate in a better way. I have a good experience in my social life. I would like to say, if you have a difficulty, try a good way to overcome it and ask for the help you need. No matter how long you spend, you will reach your goal. Don't wait too long to try some solutions. There's a lot of opportunities in Australia.

However, you need to make good decisions and work hard.

Mohamed Camara, OAE

My name is Mohamed Camara. I am from the Guinea Republic's capital city Conakry in West Africa. I am a student at Olympic Adult Education (OAE) at this moment, and I am also studying community services three days a week. I have a soccer program coaching young people skills as part of my knowledge for two hours. I do my work placement in a local organisation.

I chose to learn English because it is the first stage for me to integrate into society and also to have better skills in English writing and speaking. Having these skills I will be able to work properly in the industry that I would like to work. I know that at the moment I need to work hard to achieve my goals, but I am sure soon I will get there.

Generally I have had many different experiences in my life concerning my learning skills. Being in a new country like Australia is exciting because despite the obstacles, this country's education system is offering different opportunities to new arrivals to study English.

When I arrived in Australia two and a half years ago, I had some learning skills problems like communicating clearly with people but, since I joined Olympic Adult Education (OAE), I have improved a lot my skills in writing and speaking English.

Before, I was speaking a little bit of English but not so well as to express myself completely or to understand people properly when they speak. Now I am starting to be more relaxed when I am in conversation with people like doctors, teachers, workers or friends.

To overcome these learning challenges, the experiences I have got before were very important to me. I tried always to minimise the mistakes and to be aware of some serious points. I encouraged myself and I never gave up to achieve my goals.

Now I am still learning English and doing my courses in the community services sector. My English skills have improved a lot and probably will help me to study and understand my options for further paid work. I am doing at the moment my work placement and a volunteer job as well as to prepare my career by getting a permanent and full-time job.

By participating in adult education, I can create new relationships with co-workers, make new friends and communicate with people appropriately. I am confident in speaking English although I am not yet very good, but I can express better my ideas now than a few months ago, which is positive.

I will just encourage other people to join the adult education centres so that it will be easier for them to integrate into society, and also to find better jobs. We can say also that it will help them to create new networks which is very important for their career.

Huong Nguyen, OAE

My name is Huong Nguyen. I come from Vietnam. I was a lecturer in a university before I moved to Melbourne in February this year. In Vietnam, I studied pharmacy and worked in only one place. After one month staying at home as a housewife, I took an English course at an adult education centre. I want to find a stable job to settle down. I want to pursue a similar job as I did before. But my English limitations made it difficult to find a job. Nevertheless, the requalification fee of pharmacy is expensive for me to afford. I used to have successful work in my country; however, I have to restart my career in this foreign city. English grammar was hard for me to remember, especially the irregular verbs and the diversity of verbs and prepositions' combination.

Luckily, my family and friends instructed me to find this course and chose the nearest study place for me. Besides, my English teachers and classmates have shared unhesitatingly their knowledge and experience with me.

Until now, my English speaking and listening skills have improved. I became more confident in social communication and less dependent on my husband. I spend more time outside the house and feel relieved whenever I come to the class. I feel happy when I can tell any stranger the right direction to the bus station. One month ago, I was very reluctant to say a word because I was afraid of giving the wrong instructions.

Don't ever think it will be a waste of time to restart studying in adult education. Every moment you spend in class, you will feel relieved and upgraded. An English class is not only about English studying. I have learnt how to work out my problems gradually thanks to my class.

.:] Rubina Bhatti, Surrey Adult Learning

Multimedia

Two video clips with Rubina Bhatti are available on http://rapal.org.uk/resilience/

Rubina's Story

I am Rubina Bhatti originally from Lahore, Pakistan. I belong to a lower middle class family with strong morals. We are four sisters and one brother. We all were very bright academically. I was only eight when the sudden death of our father left us in great financial crisis along with several other problems. When I finished school I got 18th position in the whole district but it could not prolong my life as a student and I had to stop my studies because of financial problems.

In 2000, when I came to England to live with my husband, I hoped to resume my studies and pass my driving test to settle in England in a proper way. I had big dreams and also the zeal to match them but nature had different plans for me.

After a month of my arrival I got pregnant. It proved a difficult pregnancy and, to make things worse, I was supposed to do all the housework in a house of eight family members. Anyway my first baby was born and then only two and a half months later I was expecting again. My miserable condition led me to believe that I might never be able to fulfil my dreams of further education and an independent life. Lost in raising my children and looking after the family, I was oblivious to my own existence. That isolation from the external world sucked even the last drop of my self-confidence. Then almost six years later I had my third son. He was diagnosed with a speech problem when he started nursery.

One day I got a call from my son's school asking if I was interested in joining a Family Learning Language Course, as even at the age of four and half, he would scarcely say a word. I accepted that offer in the hope it might enable me to improve his speech and studies. That was how God put me back on the path of learning almost fifteen years later.

It proved a great experience for me and my family. During that course I learnt so much about the UK. It was like I never knew this country before. I learnt about the education system which changed my approach towards my children's learning. Sulaiman, my youngest son, was doing much better in class in every aspect. His growing confidence made me feel proud of my decision to join the course. I started helping my other two sons in their learning as well, which improved their grades at school. I helped my middle son in preparing for the entry tests for Reigate Grammar School on my own, as I could not afford the private tuition fees. When he passed the test I felt like I had passed. Those were the things which helped me regain my confidence and inspired me to keep up with my adult learner life.

After passing the reading module of a Level 1 Functional Skills English qualification, I did another Family Learning course and passed the writing and speaking exams to get full the Functional Skills English qualification. At the same time, I did three other courses with WEA which included Microsoft Word Skills, Helping in Schools Level 1 and 2. At the moment I am doing GCSE Maths and English (higher tier) so I can help my older sons to prepare for their GCSEs from next year.

For the last two and a half years I have been volunteering in my little son's school. I am also doing a job as a creche worker in the same school and hoping to get a job as a Teaching Assistant. My life is even busier now as I have to manage everything alongside my studies and work myself. After putting my children to bed I start doing my college work and usually stay awake until two o'clock at night.

In 2013, my family learning course class teacher nominated me for the Adult Learner Award 2014, now Festival of Learning. Thursday, 10th of June 2014 at London Canal Museum, I experienced one of the proudest moments of my life when I received an individual award for South East Learning in Families and Communities. I went there with two of my sons and my husband. In that ceremony we were surrounded by some amazing real life heroes. Their heart touching stories brought tears to our eyes and made us feel humbled and privileged. On our way back home my husband told me that it was the best event of his life. I advised my children if those people could achieve what they struggled for despite all difficulties and disabilities then you should have no excuse to not excel in life ahead. Since that day I have witnessed that they have been more serious in their attitude towards studies and life in general.

My husband doesn't get tired of saying how I and that evening have inspired him to do something good in life. He had finished his studies after GCSEs as he was never interested in academics but after that event he applied for a crash course as a Gas Safety Engineer. Amazingly within four months he has become an engineer. We both are trying to pass our driving test and planning to do some more courses in future. My husband very proudly says we are a learner family. That event had such an inspirational atmosphere to it that we still talk about it and get motivation in our lives.

In the end I would like to say that we all get only one chance to live in this world. Some live to inspire others but most of us get inspiration to live it. It is not important which category we fall in but whether we are bringing the best out of it or not. We are born as students until death, so we should never let anything come our way to success and betterment. I firmly believe that a healthy action originates from a healthy and positive thinking mind and that is the most essential thing to make this world a beautiful and peaceful place to live.

Tutor Perspective: Maria Szende

Rubina Bhatti attended a 30-week Keeping up with the Children (Language) course I ran at St Matthews Church of England Primary School in Redhill, Surrey in 2012-2013. The course was provided by Family Programmes, which is part of Surrey Adult Learning .

The main objective of Family Learning Programmes is to develop the skills of parents/carers and children together. One of the reasons why some children struggle at school may be the lack or amount of appropriate support they get with their school work at home. Family Learning courses are set up in partnership with schools and children centres who invite "targeted" families: families who will get the most benefit from the opportunity to access this kind of free learning because, for example, parents have lower academic skills or do not have English as their first language.

There are two types of courses: Wider Family Learning (WFL) and Family English, Maths and Language (FEML). WFL courses aim to encourage families to learn something together, e.g. Cooking on a Budget, Family First Aid, Managing your Money, Steps into School, etc.

FEML courses aim to help parents/carers understand how English and maths are taught at school and thus to increase their ability and confidence to support their children and to improve their own skills. They also offer learners the chance to gain qualifications (e.g. Functional Skills, OCR Progression Units) and to receive guidance on how to progress to further learning or employment.

Rubina was invited to a Family Learning Language course at St Matthews because her son, Sulaiman, was very shy and quiet in class and his teacher thought that he and his mum, whose first language is Urdu, could benefit from the opportunity of learning together. It was a "joint" course, which means that in the first ninety minutes of the session parents worked with me (Family Learning tutor) and children worked separately with a school teacher, and then there was a thirty minute joint session where parents and children worked together, e.g. sequenced a story, wrote a card, decorated a biscuit, made a finger puppet, etc.

Rubina was very keen to attend the course as she had not had the chance to do any formal learning since she arrived in the U.K. twelve years before. She had been busy raising children and looking after a rather large family where her own needs were not always given priority.

She never missed a class and always did the home activity I set for her and Sulaiman. She had a thirst for knowledge and applied everything she heard in class to improving her own and her child's skills. In addition to covering topics related to the children's learning at school and life in the U.K., parents also prepared for the reading module of the OCR Functional Skills English exam at various levels. Rubina passed the level 1 Reading module in June 2013. She attended an adult only family learning language course the following school year and passed the speaking and listening and writing modules in June 2014.

It was absolutely fascinating to see how profoundly an opportunity to learn could make someone's life change for the better: Rubina's self-esteem grew quickly and she started to feel confident enough to sit down and learn not only with Sulaiman but with her two elder sons too. A few months into her first family learning course, she said she would really like to help out at her child's school. I encouraged her to speak to Sulaiman's teacher and a few weeks later she started volunteering: she worked two days at the school reading with children and helping in the library. Soon she was asked to do three days. To be better equipped for her voluntary role, she gained level 1 and level 2 Preparing to Help in School qualifications with the Workers' Educational Association. Next she enrolled on and completed a couple of IT courses (Microsoft Word and Microsoft Excel).

Towards the end of the first family learning course, we all went on a trip to East Surrey College, which is the local further education provider. The objective of the trip is twofold: on the one hand, I would like parents to see where their children might gain qualifications in the future, on the other hand, I would like the parents to meet ESOL tutors and to learn about courses that they might be interested in. We often forget how scary it can be to walk through the doors of a huge and impressive building and to talk to staff if one's first language is not English. These visits always encourage people to come back and enrol on courses. Rubina was very interested in progressing to mainstream education and made an appointment for an assessment. In September 2014 she enrolled on her GCSE English and maths courses. She took her exams having been an outstanding student all through the year. Rubina passed her English and maths GCSEs summer 2015 and has since enrolled on a health and social care course at university.

I nominated Rubina for an individual award (Adult Learners' Week, now Festival of Learning) and she was awarded a Learning in Families and Communities Individual Regional Award (South East) in 2014. The awards ceremony in London was an unforgettable and extremely inspiring event for Rubina, her family and myself.

Her achievements and the awards ceremony have had a positive impact on her family: all her children are doing very well at school and even her husband has gone back to college and has recently gained a qualification in gas safety. Rubina has been very supportive of other students too. She always gives advice and encouragement to others. She is a fantastic role model in her community and a great example to all those who have moved to the United Kingdom and want to contribute to this society.

I feel privileged to have been able to see Rubina's transformation from being a woman whose primary task in life a little over three years ago seemed to be looking after a big family, to being a woman who is planning to train to be a social worker. Without the opportunity of attending a family learning course, Rubina may have never had the confidence to learn with her children or to talk to the school about volunteering there, let alone think about pursuing a career in social work. The opportunity presented itself when the school invited her to the course but it was up to her to make the best of that course and of further learning opportunities to progress.

Her enthusiasm for and commitment to improving her skills and then using these skills to help others are quite exceptional. I love my job and find working with adult learners very rewarding but when I have students like Rubina, I feel the most fortunate person in the world.

Shaista Aamir, South Grove Primary Family Learning

It's my pleasure to write something about learning at South Grove Primary Family Learning. I'm extremely grateful that I have had a chance to be a part of it. It's my personal experience that there is no comparison of South Grove Primary to other learning institutes because the atmosphere was really friendly, excellent teachers, and really supportive and welcoming people, who really care about learners.

I started my educational journey from South Grove. When I started my study, I wasn't able to communicate with others but my teacher was very supportive. She encouraged me to learn and speak. My kids were studying there so it was very easy for me to learn at South Grove while my kids were in school. Now I'm able to communicate with different people. I've learnt lots of things during my studies so I could balance both my study and family. I can help my kids with their homework and targets. My kids are improving a lot in their studies. I would like to thank Ms Brigid Montgomery (extended school leader). She gave me a great opportunity to run the speaking English club at South Grove. That made a huge difference in my life. Honestly speaking, I would not be as confident as I am today. This is because of learning at South Grove. I never want to leave this school although we've moved to Islington but still me and my kids are studying in this school. I would highly recommend South Grove to everyone (both kids and adults). Thank you so much South Grove for giving me such big opportunities.

Yuliya Yankova, South Grove Primary Family Learning

For people like me, who came to the UK from another country, it is very important to improve their language, to be able to work and participate appropriately in the English community.

South Grove School offered to parents many different courses to help them in their everyday life. I had a chance to attend all these courses with absolutely no cost for me.

They gave me an opportunity to learn English and maths and to gain new skills as a teaching assistant. All the teachers were trained, competent and friendly professionals, who were able to respond to everyone's needs.

I am very happy that I participated in all those classes because I found lots of good friends from all over the world and the most important is that I am able to communicate freely with all of them.

.:] Tutor Perspective: Brigid Montgomery

Multimedia

A video clip with Brigid Montgomery is available on http://rapal.org.uk/resilience/

Learning Together Project

This project aims to improve the educational attainment and aspirations of the extended family members of South Grove Primary school and offers opportunities to increase their confidence through a varied learning offer thus increasing a sense of community cohesion and an improved adult knowledge of local training, learning and volunteering. Our school is situated in Markhouse ward in Walthamstow, East London and the ward is in the top 5% of multiple deprivation nationally. There are forty-four different community languages spoken in the school. Many of our families face complex challenges relating to isolation, mental health, poverty, language, fear of crime and emotional and social issues. As a school our primary aim is to raise the literacy and numeracy of children but we recognise the vital role of parents in supporting their children's learning too.

Our project has offered a variety of classes and sessions including Adult literacy, ESOL, Parenting, Family English, and Childcare and teaching assistant courses, Family Yoga, African dance and drumming, Tai Chi, Gardening, Circus skills and a book celebrating our diverse cultures. Some of the softer options act as a hook to encouraging people to try something new with their children or other adults. We always consult and speak with parent learners about learning pathways that they may find useful. Using this information and local health, crime and educational data helps us to plan our activities. This makes it easier to respond to local need. We work in partnership with adult providers like the WEA and Waltham Forest adult learning to provide classes and then identify pockets of funding which enable a variety of active and more creative sessions for families. This is an on-going process.

We use a mobile classroom within the school for classes and we provide a creche where possible to enable parents to engage in learning as soon as their youngest child is one year old. This has meant that the adults feel comfortable as they know the school building and that childcare is offered to encourage early engagement with learning. Word of mouth works well when promoting classes as well as flyers etc which are publicised locally.

The outcomes from this project are very noticeable. School staff report better and closer communication with families. There has been an increase in parents volunteering to help with school activities, new friendships have been formed and there is a greater focus on learning. However, it is the outcomes for the learners and their families that is most obvious. Some learners have progressed from ESOL classes to working as teaching assistants in primary and secondary schools. Others have progressed to college courses in hairdressing and office skills. Some have gone on to work in retail and catering. Two learners completed a training course, which means that they volunteer to host English conversation classes for other newly arrived parents.

Adults who attend our classes have had a variety of difficult life experiences including domestic violence, depression, asylum seeking, challenging previous relationships with schools, and education which has impacted on their confidence but the retention and development of the learners within this project is clear. There are a small group of learners who do not have even basic literacy skills and we are trying to engage with this group currently.

It may be helpful to hear some of the feedback we have had.

Parent who completed a parenting course:

"This course should be taken by ALL parents, not just because it reassures you that some of the things you are doing are correct but it also gives you the skills and tools to work with your children in this community and time, which may be so different from the one you grew up in. This parenting class taught me more about the different cultures which make up this community and the similarities with regards to our families and the problems we may have with our children. Now that I have completed the course, I am more empowered and prepared to work with my children on any issue and I'm looking forward to helping them develop into positive and strong individuals."

Conversation with JR aged 8 (after a course of Family Juggling) that she completed with her mother who has had mental health issues:

"At the beginning my mum couldn't even catch a ball. She learnt how to catch and throw a juggling ball. I learnt how to juggle with two balls, walk on stilts, balance on the pedals... My favourite is the diablo and we learnt to do the wavy things with scarves.

You could play on anything and James (the teacher) was really nice and you could ask him anything and even if you did not ask he would see that you needed help. My mum and me learnt from him. Most of all it was just really good fun and it meant my mum did something with me."

Comment from an adult volunteer:

"I can not believe how much I have learnt here. I can now speak and write English. I have made friends and know that I can do anything. My husband always said that I had a worm in my brain which made me stupid. This is not true. I want to help this school and other women."

I would like finally quote one of the learners from a book about the school:

"Secondly, I would like to thank my friends who helped me on this project and for sharing a wonderful moment together"

We are determined to share many more moments within this school community.

Trinh Tien Mui, MTC Bankstown

Refugee from Vietnam - Hong Kong and then to Australia

I left Vietnam in 1978 with my husband and my two daughters on a small boat. I could not remember how many people were on the boat, but we couldn't move and there were not enough seats. We were scared that the boat was going to turn over or sink. It was very risky.

At that time our daughters were very young: one was one year old and the other one was two years old. The journey on a small boat lasted one day until the next day, when we got rescued by a big ship with plenty of other small boats in the ocean waiting to be rescued at the same time.

After the rescue, the big ship carried a total of two thousand people, arriving in Hong Kong. We stayed in a camp and we had some freedom. My husband found a job in Hong Kong and I stayed in the hut, looking after my children, shopping and cooking for my family. Sometimes we went on picnics.

We stayed in a refugee camp for three and a half years and then my sister who lived in Australia sponsored my family to come to Australia and here we are! My family feels very lucky and happy to be here and I love life. My grandchildren make me laugh when they come to visit me.

Dennis Shum, Glenroy Neighbourhood Learning Centre

Resilience...

In 1977, for my first steps in Australia, a lot of my family told me not to worry about English, because here were so many Chinese shops that I can go shopping by myself without English, and I can just work in a Chinese cafe in the kitchen. That is why I can live here very well with my poor English. I had my own business as well, where both my sons helped me.

Five years ago, I had to finish my business and sell my shop because my sons have their new goals. They don't want to work at the restaurant forever. After I finished my business, I tried to go to Centrelink and told them that I had no job. At this time I found I was so useless to do anything. When Centrelink interviewed me, I had to use the interpreter to help. Then the Centrelink people said to me, why not come back to school again and learn some English. At first I was so scared. I thought that a fifty-eight year old man still can learn. I did as they suggested.

I started going to school, learning writing and speaking English. I kept doing it for about a year. One day, I got an appointment at Centrelink, but they didn't give me the interpreter and they said: "Do it yourself." With a no-choice situation, I just tried to do it. After the interview, the Centrelink staff said that my English is not too bad. I understand 'not too bad' means still bad. I know my English journey still has a long way to go, but who cares; I will keep going to school and keep learning.

Sometimes when the Centrelink staff say to me, "your English is better than before", I feel so confident. Another confidence is that I can go shopping to a lot of shops; many kinds of shops, not only Chinese ones. Also I can ask the shopkeeper what I want and they can show me where to get it.

I find that my world is getting bigger. I'm happier than before.

I remember one of the stupid sayings is: "learning has no ending." It looks so funny, but it's true. So I choose to follow it. I know this is the only way to re-birth myself. It is another kind of power.

Hulya Yorur, Glenroy Neighbourhood Learning Centre

Journey To My Confidence

At the age of nineteen we moved to Australia from Turkey. When we arrived I knew very basic English but it wasn't enough to make friends or even talk to people on the street, so I started English classes. But after one year my dad decided that it was time for me to get married so he arranged for my cousin, who lived overseas, to come to Australia and marry me. It wasn't easy but I accepted my dad's wishes and married my cousin. But sadly, the marriage meant the end of my education as well.

After twenty years, when my youngest started school, I started to feel differently about staying home and not doing anything for myself or for the community. All the strong and positive feelings that I had been feeling as a stay-at-home mum started to disappear. I started to feel lonely, depressed, sad and started to feel sorry for myself as well.

But one morning when I went to pick up my mail from the letter box, I saw this flyer about neighbourhood English classes. I never thought that flyer would change my life.

I told my family and my friends about the classes and the first thing that they said to me was: "What are you going to do in English classes? Your English is enough to get around and you also have responsibilities at home. Don't worry about the language too much."

After thinking about it all night and making lots of excuses not to enrol in the classes, I finally made the decision to enrol because deep down I knew that the only way that I can really communicate with people is if I knew the language well. Next morning I woke up and went straight to Glenroy Neighbourhood House and enrolled myself.

In the English classes at first I was the quiet one. I always kept to myself and didn't ask any questions. But the Glenroy Neighbourhood staff and the teachers were so helpful that slowly I started to blossom. At the end of two years, I was the student who was asking a lot of questions and started to have confidence and make lots of friends.

The teachers were so happy with my progress that they asked me to do a voluntary program involving teaching English at home to newly-arrived refugees. Also, I had the confidence to enrol in a computer class. Around the same time, I started to volunteer for St John's ambulance to be a first-aider and help the community, which I enjoyed doing very much.

To this day, I am still volunteering at the Neighbourhood Centre by helping the migrants in the English classes, computer classes, and interpreting as well. But the important thing is, I am still continuing to do lots of different courses to improve myself.

Mariana Caruso, Glenroy Neighbourhood Learning Centre

To be resilient

My husband and I arrived in Australia in June 1958. The first few years my life wasn't too easy, because I was an immigrant from Italy and I didn't have the opportunity to study English before I left. When I arrived in Australia I was only seventeen years old. The first negative impact was the barrier of language. The first three years we lived on the farm. I had not a chance to learn the language because there wasn't an English class for adult immigrants. Luckily my husband spoke enough English to attend to what we needed.

The first problem began when I was pregnant, to talk to my doctor, and in hospital when the baby was born. When my little girl was eight months, we had to come to Melbourne because the produce we had grown had not been sold. I didn't have a job. I didn't know the language. I had the little girl to look after. I got a job through a friend. I have learned to use sewing machines. It was not easy for me.

When I was pregnant with the second child, it was very difficult. I had a bad pregnancy. I could not work. We had bought a house, and we had to pay the mortgage. I bought a sewing machine. I started to work at home for a company producing garments for women. I did that for twenty-five years. The work wasn't paid well. I worked long hours with little profit. It has been a very stressful period, taking care of the little one, bringing and taking the oldest from school. Ten years later I had another child. This time was easier.

When my husband died, my two oldest two daughters were married and the youngest still went to university, so I needed to work to support her. For me, it was the worst time of my life. I didn't drive cars, so the first thing I had to do was learn to drive. For me, it wasn't easy at the age of fifty-eight years. Because I needed it, I had to become stronger and force myself to achieve that. Four years later, I woke up with the intention to help myself to change my attitude. First, I needed to learn to drive, so I took my learning permit, and started driving lessons. I had to do five driving tests before I had my driving licence. I was very proud of myself for having the courage and strength to reach this goal.

After this success, my life took a different turn. I could go to see my daughters, pass time and spoil my grandchildren, visit my friends, and attend to all the things I needed. After my youngest daughter married, I stopped working. I was very tired. I needed to have some rest. Now, I have more time for myself. I'm going to English classes, as well computer classes, at my age of seventy-five years old. Never is it too late to learn.

Rita Lin, Glenroy Neighbourhood Learning Centre

Story of Resilience

My name is Rita. My story began a long time ago back in Taiwan. I was married and had two little children. My husband was a mechanic and owned a garage. With the business and the family, it kept us very busy.

One day, strangely, a primary school friend who I had lost contact with for many years somehow found me. Living in America, she encouraged us to move overseas because mechanics are a very special skill. She suggested New Zealand, which coincidently was open for immigration at that time. Once we got accepted, we lost contact with her again. It seemed she just appeared to make us move, which we had never thought of.

We started a very new and totally different life in New Zealand. It was very hard, scary and difficult at the beginning. My children were small, so they didn't have problems with English soon after attending school, but my husband and I really struggled.

Every day, I would learn English with my children when they were doing their homework. I also forced myself to listen to the language by watching TV. I tried to talk to people if I had the chance. Some time later, I found a part-time job during school hours that enabled me to practice my English. I was a bookkeeper in Taiwan, but here I worked as a kitchen hand, a packer, a jewellery waxer and a dispatch person due to my poor English. While I was at work, I could see my English was improving day by day. I could understand what people said and I could talk more.

For twenty years we lived in New Zealand: my children grew up and graduated there. My husband did open a garage. Sadly, it didn't last long. We loved New Zealand and thought it would be our second home country, until something strange happened again. My husband bought an old Austin Healey car. Because he felt there was no company that specialises in restoring these, he sent the car to The Healey Factory in Melbourne. We followed the car and moved again, to Melbourne.

Soon after we moved, my children and husband fortunately all found jobs. I tried to find a part-time job as well but was not successful. I even attended a training school to get a Certificate III in Financial Services to help, but there was still no luck for me. I thought maybe it was because of my English, so now I am studying English here at Glenroy Neighbourhood Learning Centre. Because of my age, I am no longer looking for a job any more. I'm happy learning English here and enjoy it very much. Life to me now is much easier and less stressful.

I am proud of what I have done in my life so far. I can now read and communicate in spoken and written English with people. I think it is never too late to learn English. Resilience has made me stronger and tougher.

Nguyet Tran, Glenroy Neighbourhood Learning Centre

My life story

My name is Nguyet Tran. I was born in Saigon, Vietnam. My family was middle class. My father was a business man. I have three brothers. I started school in 1961 and finished high school in 1974. After I finished high school, I did accountancy at university but didn't finish. In 1975 the communists came. We wanted freedom, so I left my country by boat in 1981. For the first time, I went to a refugee camp in Indonesia. I lived there until 1983. Then I came to Australia on the 15 March 1983.

In July 1983 I started my job as a quality checker for dresses. I changed many jobs like sewing, packing etc. I got married 1984. I have a daughter and a son. In 1989, I got a good job at Yakka. I used to cut clothes by computer. I worked there until 2006. I retired because I was sick. I had many troubles when I could not speak English well. If I went to a doctor or a hospital, I need my kid's help, but they were busy with their jobs. I decided to come to school and learn English. So, I came to GNLC. Now, I understand the news on TV and I can watch the news every day. I have the confidence to go to a doctor and a hospital by myself. I can socialize and I have made new friends. I am very happy in Australia. I feel I have a good retired life.

.:] Qianghua Chen Anne, Glenroy Neighbourhood Learning Centre

Multimedia

⊙ An audio interview between Qianghua Chen Anne and Michael Chalk is available on http://rapal.org.uk/resilience/, with accompanying transcript.

Anne's Story

My story. I am Anne. I come from China. I have been in Australia for two years. I like to tell you my story to learn English. In China, I am a maths teacher in high school. I taught maths for thirty years. We used computers in home teaching. I also wrote teaching methods books. My students are working in Australia, and in America and England. In China, I am a bit important. I felt I was a very useful person, so no time to learn English. My English was zero.

After I came here, everywhere is in English. My eyes couldn't see, my mouth couldn't speak, my ears couldn't hear, and my hands couldn't write. I felt I was a useless person. I couldn't shop, I couldn't take the bus, I couldn't go out, and I couldn't tell my story to you. I was not happy. I hadn't any friends.

And then I came to Glenroy Neighbourhood Learning Centre to learn English in Manjit's class. I got all the help now. I can speak a little English. I can go shopping. I can take the bus to go out. I can tell my story to you. I like it here. Now I am feeling happy. My teacher Manjit has raised me up.

.:] Jian San Wang, Glenroy Neighbourhood Learning Centre

Multimedia

⦿ An audio interview between Jian San Wang and Michael Chalk is available on http://rapal.org.uk/resilience/, with accompanying transcript.

Jian San Wang's Story

My name is Jian San. I come from China. I didn't know English. I was meeting people in the street, I didn't know words, so I felt embarrassed. After learning English here, I love meeting people in the street. I know they are talking to me. I feel great now. I feel comfortable.

Rose, Glenroy Neighbourhood Learning Centre

I was born in Vietnam, but my parents are Chinese, so I speak Cantonese. After Vietnam had divided into two countries, South Vietnam and North Vietnam, the civil war began. Later on North Vietnam took over South Vietnam and united north and south, and they became one nation, the communist country. The people in the south, because of different policies, escaped Vietnam to seek freedom.

Together with my parents, young brother and two cousins, we left Vietnam. It was very dark and I saw a lot of people were waiting to get into a vessel at the beach. Those seven nights and eight days for me were a very extremely terrible period of time. When the vessel began to sail, some people started to vomit. After two days, the vessel nearly sailed into international waters. The captain saw a vessel was going towards our vessel. All of us were very happy. But unfortunately, that was a pirate ship. When the pirate's ship was close to our vessel, the pirates started to shoot machine guns into the sky, tried to warn us not to move until the pirates jumped into our vessel. The pirates wanted to find our expensive things. For example: diamond, gold, American dollars. After they found a lot of expensive things they felt very happy. At that time, I was frightened because they had a terrible face. They looked like Captain Hook who acted in the movie, but it was a real person.

Time went by. I arrived in Australia. It was morning, about 7 o'clock on 17th of July in 1980. I felt very cold. I was on the bus. I saw the road was very quiet and the houses were exposed to bricks that were around the house. I wanted to go back to Vietnam, but now I like Australia.

.:] Ming Zheng, Glenroy Neighbourhood Learning Centre

Multimedia

⦿ An audio interview between Ming Zheng and Michael Chalk is available on http://rapal.org.uk/resilience/, with accompanying transcript.

Ming Zheng's Story

My story. My name is Ming. I came from China in 1998 with my husband and my son. My family all came here. First life in Australia was very difficult, so the first thing was to make a living.

Previously in my country, I was a maths teacher. But coming to Australia, my English was not good. So previous experience... I couldn't do it. So, I had to do physical labour.

My son finished university. I can learn English now. I am retired. I learn English in the Glenroy Neighbourhood Learning Centre. If I am like the deaf and the blind and the dumb, my life is very inconvenient, so I am determined to learn English. My teacher is Manjit. Manjit taught us very well, so I have been in the English conversation class. Now, I have been learning nearly three years. Now, I can go to shopping. I can ask the price, where something is - I can ask. Sometimes I go to hospital. I can have a conversation with the doctor - simple. For example, I lost my filling. I can speak - simple. Then I can go out, by tram, by bus, and now, I can see my friends, greeting to everyone.

I usually learn English by learning grammar in the home by myself, but in the class I practise speaking, listening. I think I've improved. Now Manjit, if he says something, I understand. I feel very happy. Stronger than before. The first time, I was very sad, very worried. I couldn't speak, couldn't listen. Now I am strong. Now I am very happy.

.:] Jian Kui Peng, Glenroy Neighbourhood Learning Centre

Multimedia

⊙ An audio interview between Jian Kui Peng and Michael Chalk is available on http://rapal.org.uk/resilience/, with accompanying transcript.

Jian Kui Peng's Story

My name is Jian Kui Peng. I come from China. I came to Australia for my family because I have three sons; they are all in Australia. So, I and my wife came to Australia for a family reunion. In the beginning, coming to Australia, everything for me was very strange. Everything I didn't know.

Then, slowly, I came to Glenroy Neighbourhood Learning Centre, to learn English, the AMEP English – 510 hours class. Then it was strange to know something, to look at something. I can to a poor man for a daughter. I can go shopping. I can catch the bus and train. I can talk with neighbours, for connecting with communities. For my spirit, I am very happy; not alone, very alone. Now I can connect with other people, with the community. I am very happy. It is slow, learning English in the Learning Centre, as a family. We learn English. We learn with each other, learn in the group.

Life for me is very happy; not at home alone for me, only for me and my wife. Because my son goes to work, he is not at home. I came to this school for many classmates, many schoolmates, brothers and sisters as a family. We are learning with each other. We help each other. We are very happy. I learn English to enrich my life and my spirit. Always to use my brain, I can avoid some sickness. This brain has always to be used.

.:] Zhiyuan Cheng, Glenroy Neighbourhood Learning Centre

Multimedia

⊙ An audio interview between Zhiyuan Cheng and Michael Chalk is available on http://rapal.org.uk/resilience/, with accompanying transcript.

Zhiyuan Cheng's Story

My story. I am from China. I was working in a shipping company for international shipping. I learnt English in China in night school, like college. Then I used some English during my working life. I had to send cable, send fax and some things in English to the other companies overseas. Usually I can write and read some English but listening and speaking is not good.

I came here as my son is working here. I found I could not hear. Some people's English I could understand but in Australia most people come from everywhere around the world. It is just like the U.N. with so many different accents, including mine. I speak English: other people cannot understand me and I cannot understand others as well. I can read and I can write some, and then they can understand me. So, I came here to learn English, and to correct my accent, and to understand other people with different accents. My memory is not so good. I learn a word here. Tomorrow I will forget it. So, I have to keep my mind and my English fresh.

I was taking a train and the announcement that the train stopped, I couldn't understand it. Other passengers were getting off the train and I couldn't understand. I asked the other passengers what happened. They said that the driver told us the train will not go further. They have to stop here and they have some trouble. So, everybody has to get off the train and then take the bus to go on. So, I hope I can learn more English and understand other people so I can understand what the announcements say so I cannot get lost.

.:] Mohua Wang, Glenroy Neighbourhood Learning Centre

Multimedia

⦿ An audio interview between Mohua Wang, his tutor Manjit Bhamral, and Michael Chalk is available on http://rapal.org.uk/resilience/, with accompanying transcript.

Mohua Wang's Story

I came to Australia in 1994. My name is Mohua. Before I came from China, Beijing, I was working in the Beijing Telecommunications Institute. I designed computer equipment for telecommunications. I was a telecommunications engineer. I did this work for twenty-nine years. Then I came to Australia. My English was no good, so I couldn't do this work. I couldn't do anything. The time I came here, twenty-two years ago, I learned English, but I couldn't do it well, so sometimes I felt life was difficult. I see my daughter. I can't listen. I can't answer.

So I like learning English.

A few years ago, I came here, learning English for Manjit. I feel my English is improved, so I like to continue learning. I like this class. I like continuing learning. If they make more time, that will be better I think. My grandson goes to school, comes back and talks English, I don't understand, so that feels difficult. I am older, so it's difficult. But I like learning... and yes, I like coming to class.

.:] Tutor Perspective: Manjit Bhamral

Actually, last term when we were talking about this class, they were telling me that they come here to learn English but also that they come here to meet each other. Life is quite lonely or difficult or a challenge. Then they come here and they forget so many things or they are one with each other. Then they make different programs, sometimes also out of class, to go somewhere sometimes. Through this class, coming to know each other, they join other groups as a result. It's so good for their self-esteem, coming here. Just before you came, we were talking. There's not such a huge jump in my English but here I feel good, just to be at peace, meeting other people, seeing that other people face similar challenges. It takes a lot of courage to talk.

Very difficult when you don't have the language because, when I am doing a lot of speaking activities, I can see in your eyes you understand but it's not coming out because you don't have the language. You're all adults and so many of you are older than me and you've got life experiences which (you) share with me. It's just the language that hinders.: very challenging.

From my experience of learning a language, when I came to Australia, I had the language but I felt like I was Somebody in my country and I was Nobody here. It took a lot of time and patience to become Somebody. Now, I know people know my name. Now, I know that when I go somewhere, people come and talk to me. Before, I would be in a crowd and nobody knew me and I knew nobody. It was a very strange feeling. I found Australia to be very big and vast and I was lost. I was lost. It's the same Australia but I have an identity now, so I understand what you say (Mohua).

.:] Mark Hopkins, PRACE Education and Training

Multimedia

⦿ An audio interview between Mark Hopkins and Michael Chalk is available on http://rapal.org.uk/resilience/, with accompanying transcript.

Mark's Story

I suppose you've got to go right back to the start. I was fifteen and a half when I left school, and I can relate to a student who struggles. It is hard when you go through school, and you are the class idiot and you can't do the basic things. It wasn't my own decision to leave school, but my parents didn't see the point of me trying to accomplish VCE when my report card would turn up with UG "ungradeable" on it. My father was of the opinion that we would be better off taking me out of school and learning a trade or something. It's very hard in the country when there are just no opportunities. The nearest TAFE was forty minutes away and I didn't drive.

It was difficult growing up in a country town. You tend to know everyone. The hardest time for me was when I left school. A lot of people saw me on the street and said, "Where have you been?" I was vague, and tended to hide from society, because I was ashamed of the circumstances I was in. So when I came to the city, through contacts I found some employment. It was an average job, but you're gracious enough to take whatever you can get. After a few months I knew this type of employment wasn't going to be the future I wanted. So, I decided to return to school.

It wasn't easy at first, going back to school and trying to study again, but I knew I had to do it. I had to be committed to it. I was working a shift job, so I would leave after a twelve hour night shift then go to school, but by eleven o'clock I was falling asleep and my teacher would wake me up and would send me home. Then I made the ultimate sacrifice and attempted to find another job, which was very scary for me. I finally achieved getting another job so I could start night school. I reduced my work hours from twelve to eight. Money was a bit of an issue, but for me it was about looking toward the future.

I would apply myself for two to three hours a night over the week plus go to school as well. I was continually reading and writing with all the work going to my teacher. I have a lot of very thick folders at home with all my work in them. Sometimes you get frustrated and you say to yourself, "I'm not improving," but then you'll go back and look over your work from a year ago and I could say to myself, "Yes, you are improving!"

Turning up for two hours is a good start, but you really need to try and do more at home. I enjoy writing. It's something I can do to improve my English. I find it a bit of escapism, and I quite enjoy it. The more you do, the more you will improve.

I have been lucky. I've done a few adult literacy courses before. I had a lady at TAFE. Her name was Sophie and I spent five years with her, and due to family reasons she couldn't continue to do nights any more. Then another teacher came in and the chemistry changed. Her approach was very different and unfortunately it didn't suit me. After three months, she told us all that she had to leave. Then we got a fill-in teacher. We kept getting multiple teachers and the chemistry wasn't there anymore. So I decided to have a break.

You never give up though, and I had a break for a little while, and then I said to myself that I needed to go back. I started to ring around and track down some places. I went back to the TAFE again, but they concentrated on ESL (English as a Second Language) now. They didn't have a level of adult literacy that suited me.

A lot of the places I used to know, or looked into, had changed their ways or shut down. Someone I called recommended PRACE to me. So, I gave them a call and had a conversation in regards to what I was looking for and after the conversation, I enrolled. On the first night I was nervous but after I met Tina, who was the English teacher, my nerves quickly disappeared.

Tina's great. She is a fantastic teacher and I would say we have a very good friendship as well.

I don't expect to be a genius or anything, but for me to have a constant source of work, I needed to improve my English, because whatever you're like at spelling or reading in today's society you're going to have to use a computer or do some sort of paperwork at home or at work. It's a part of life. You can't hide from it. I made a commitment to myself. Believe me, there were nights I'd rather have watched TV or played computer games, but at the end of the day they're just excuses. You have to be committed to what you do. I'm only kidding myself if I turn up and don't do the work, or if I don't commit to the program.

You've got to ask yourself what you want, and I don't just want to be picking up boxes or driving a forklift for the rest of my life, because I know I'm getting older, and one day my body won't be able to take it anymore. Whether those dreams turn out to be true, who knows, but at least I can say I gave it a go!

This is why I came back, because I want to self-develop. It would be great someday, if by some miracle I could turn around and help kids who were in the same situation. Deep down, I know how it feels, how tough it is. It's great when new students come in and give it a go. It helps when you have someone like Tina, who is grateful for the work that you do and she encourages you. I feel comfortable giving her my work. She doesn't give me too much help. She likes me to figure things out for myself, but she's also there if I get stuck and she will help me out. I think for anyone who is thinking about returning to school, you've got to be committed. It's about me developing enough so that one day if I want to try and look at a promotion at work or if I would like to try something else, I'll be able to.

In 2009 I had the confidence to go back to TAFE and completed a supply chain management course. In class, academically, I could answer all the questions right. I got through it and I passed. I think they were a bit intrigued by me, because in presentations they would give me 100%, but putting things on paper was the tricky bit, but ten years ago I couldn't have attempted anything like this and I wanted to do it on my own. I don't want to ask for assistance because I know that in the real world, I'm not going to get it. In the workplace I've got to do it on my own. It sounds vicious, but it's the reality.

Improving my English has also helped me in my workplace in many different ways. It gives you self-confidence. I have been the HSR (Health and Safety Representative) for over three years now. Sometimes you'll have to read things out. I was terrified of that kind of thing in the past. Now, I've got more confidence to do things like that. I will get the paper first and read through it. At least I can read through it now. Maybe there are a couple of words I mightn't understand, but I will use technology that tells me the word. When I left school, I couldn't put two words together. I was illiterate. It's difficult for anyone who's a young person, who doesn't understand the world and is faced with the biggest uphill battles. That's why I can see people like that getting depressed and down-and-out. It's building confidence in yourself. I was very fortunate in that I had good parents who supported me all the way. A lot of kids don't have that support. I was lucky in that respect.

Anyone who's contemplating an adult literacy course, just go for it. You meet some great people in an adult literacy class. I am really comfortable because everyone there understands the problem. It's not like going to a normal school. Everyone's got the same problem as you, and there's a real bonding that goes on. Don't be nervous, because the people around you have similar stories to you, and they understand. So, I say make the most of it.

I'm turning forty this year, and I've got a long road ahead of me, but no matter what happens I won't stop learning. I'll just keep going.

If anyone is thinking about it, I'd say there's no harm in trying. Not everyone's going to say it suits them, but I think everybody's also got to set themselves a goal too, to give themselves an hour or two every night. It's hard because people have families and commitments, but you've got an hour there somewhere. Lock yourself in a room, use technology to help you, like an iPad, and just commit to it. It's a slow process, don't get me wrong, but you'll see some reward. Not a piece of paper, not a promotion, but just in yourself you'll start seeing some reward.

I've met too many people who've had this problem at school, and they're so down. One of the students who is there now, John, he doesn't realise it but the change I've seen in him is fantastic. I remember when I met him two years ago, and he could hardly read. Now he's at the stage where he can read a basic book. It's the start of a chain reaction; he'll get better and better. He's sixty-three. Why does he do it? Because at the end of the day he says, "You're never too old to learn." That's so true.

Technology has been one of the big factors for me in the last ten years. I believe whatever you can use in your life to make your life easier, you should use it. I didn't just work on my reading and writing but also explored technology that might be able to assist me. I started using Dragon "natural speaking" technology. It would enable me to speak into a microphone and the words would come up on the screen. These were the days before smart phones or Siri. This gave me great independence and actually started to make me feel like a human. These days I have many apps that help me with my English.

Through the years of experience, I have been able to help many of the students with understanding the benefits of technology and I have seen so many of them smile. To see the joy on their faces when they also had the chance to have some independence of their own was very rewarding. There's a woman in my class in her fifties, who gave me a present because she said, "Understanding how these programs work has changed my life forever."

We all wish we could click our fingers and make our problems go away and I can remember the times at school and the struggle I had, but when you're knocked down enough in your life, you have to get up and get back in the ring and have another go. There is a dark side to it. You have moments where you just want to sit in the corner; emotionally it gets to you. You've got to try and pull it all together and believe there is light at the end of the tunnel, but it's not easy at times. But it is fantastic to have the support of a place like PRACE and a teacher like Tina.

So don't hide from it any more. Give it a go. Some people would say that winning is everything in life, but ask yourself this question. What determines a winner? Someone who comes first or someone who has a go?

Marion Candy, NAViGO Health and Social Care CIC

My name is Marian. My childhood days were not happy ones. When I was at school I was bullied because I was an underachiever. It was not just by the children. It was teachers as well. I was constantly told that I was thick, stupid and would not amount to anything. When I asked for help, I did not get it and was left to my own devices. So, I did nothing or say anything because I was not listened to.

The teacher was mainly concentrating on the achievers and did not give a damn about the underachievers, so I came away from school with no qualifications and I swore I would never, ever go to college or school again because I thought all teachers were the same, bullies and intimidating.

In 1983 I got married to a wonderful man called Pete. We had three children together. We both had lots of health issues and I lost both my legs due to diabetes and then we found out that my husband had got throat cancer. He then had to have a laryngectomy. In 2004 he passed away. My life was turned upside down. I had lots of problems with my children and it got to the stage where I did not want to carry on. I wanted to slit my wrists and end my life so I could be with Pete.

I was referred to Harrison house, which is part of NAViGO Health and Social Care mental health services, and got counselling and was given a support worker. It was she who took me to Tukes, which is also a part of NAViGO, and which I found to be a lovely place to be.

When I started there I had to do some assessments which were screening to dyslexia, visual stress, numeracy and literacy with the Tukes Education Team. I was then asked if I wanted to do numeracy and literacy courses. I replied by telling them to 'bugger off' on a number of occasions. However, my teacher did not bugger off. Over several months and lots of cups of coffees during my breaks, and lots of chatting, I finally succumbed and agreed to do a literacy course. Even so, I was dreading it. This was because I was told I was thick and stupid by my old teacher, so I thought I was.

I had left school at the age of sixteen years old. I had been told by teachers and continued to believe I was thick and stupid for the next thirty-five years. I had gone through my adult life, marrying, having children and bringing up a family, ill-health and becoming a widow at the age of fifty. My life was about to change. From being told I was stupid and thick, people were now saying, no you're not stupid, no you're not thick and you can do it. Others believed in me. This belief would eventually give me belief in myself and my confidence back. The only thing I didn't have to do at the age of fifty was wear a school uniform. Thank goodness, I don't think it would fit!

I found the tutor was amazing. He helped me big time by helping me break down the barriers from my past schooldays and by helping me build my confidence and my self-esteem because it was at an all-time low. He was very, very supportive throughout and continues to be. The lessons were so different, interesting, exiting and I was treated as a person.

I was gobsmacked. I actually enjoyed it and found it very rewarding. To my amazement and my teachers surprise I agreed to go on to the next level and also take maths classes. From that stage I haven't stopped and continue to enjoy learning (to my amazement and my family's).

By being in his classes I have gone from entry level literacy to level 2 literacy and numeracy. I have a certificate in mental health first aid and have also completed a PTLLS introductory teaching course. This has given me great confidence as I now work alongside the tutor as a classroom assistant. I provide learners support when they need it and can also help my grandchildren when they need help. This gives me a great sense of satisfaction, knowing that I can help and support others. I now know how my confidence is built on how things can change, no matter what stage you are at in life.

I can't thank my support worker at NAViGO Mental Health enough for introducing me to Tukes. I love it; I now know learning is all about how you are treated as a person. If others have confidence in you, you start to gain confidence in yourself.

It's all about trusting your teachers, so listen to what your friends say about how the teaching is and if they praise it, please, please give it a go. It can change your whole life. Education can be fantastic!

.:] Bulend Murad, Crisis

Multimedia

⊙ Video clips and audio by Bulend Murad, including talking about his experience with dyslexia, are available on http://rapal.org.uk/resilience/

Bulend's Story

Going back to my school days I was not the brightest pupil. I have to be honest: in the classroom I was useless. I hated English. I hated maths and I couldn't draw! But, outside the classroom it was a totally different story. I had a talent with sport. I seemed to do really well at it.

As I was growing up I got into reading short books and I quite enjoyed them. As I got older I got into more teenager books and again quite enjoyed reading in my own space. When I got to secondary school, that's when all the problems started. I just couldn't adapt to the books the class was reading and it was a real struggle. I wasn't at school for very long. I kept missing classes for a while then gave up education and got a job in a garage doing all sorts of work except reading and writing. So, that went on from thirteen years of age till I was seventeen. I decided to go back to college. I went and did a computer course because I did have good knowledge on computers and it would be a good starting point for me to get back into education.

When I was doing the course I was doing well. Not just well, really well. So that went on from 1993 – 1995. Also, during that time I was confronted with a big problem. I was struggling with English and maths. There was this one time where the tutor asked us to do a piece of writing, just a paragraph, on a piece of hardware. I didn't have a clue what to do so I found a computer book, found a paragraph on a piece of hardware and memorised it. When it came to the exam I wrote what was in the book and failed. I ended up leaving in 1995.

The problem was getting to me so much that I had to get help. I went for counselling for several years but nothing. Tried hypnosis but had no luck. I couldn't work out why I could be top at so many things but when it came to reading etc, I was struggling. But at the same time I did focus on my strong points, which were doing sport. Then when I went to the G.P. and asked for help, I was sent to see a specialist. The specialist asked me three questions and put me under mental health as schizophrenic. So before I was given that label by a specialist I was a trained martial artist, trained to end a fight within three seconds. I had a full car licence and a full bike licence and I had a girlfriend and all that was taken away from me with three questions. Shortly after I went to see a psychiatrist and he said to me, "you're schizophrenic but we don't know what it is. It's a bit like Jekyll and Hyde. You will be on medication for the rest of your life and you're not allowed to drive or ride." Between then and now I haven't been told much more about schizophrenia.

Shortly after that, I was moved out from the family home because of problems with being bullied and spent the next three years in hostels. I moved to the flat I'm still in today in 2000, which is in supported housing with support workers. I had a lot of challenges with this, was very unhappy and not making progress, and there were many changes of support workers. I stayed indoors at home for years, making my appointments with psychiatrists and psychologists. I knew I would like to get a volunteering job on a farm. It's something I have wanted to do for a long time. It's something that doesn't really involve reading or writing, so as long as I can count how many chickens there are, I should be good at the job. With a support worker, we made a list of five farms to visit. One of them was Spitalfield City Farm but at the time we didn't make any progress on this.

I went to volunteer in a cycling group at Homerton Hospital because I wanted to see the other side of the NHS. There are two sides to everything and it was no different to being a patient but I did enjoy being involved with the cycling group. The NHS stopped funding the cycling group after one year and it came to an end.

When I got a phone call to come to Crisis, I stopped all support and it's been like that since. I mentioned to my neighbour once that I wanted to do English and maths courses but I didn't want to go to college. Because he's a Crisis member, he passed my details on to Annette at Crisis and she called me to come in for a chat. Annette is the first person to give me real individualised help and I am very grateful to her. She taught me how to use grammar and punctuation and she taught me how to write. It was the same with maths. If I had a problem I couldn't work out, then Annette would sit with me and break the problem down in a way that was understandable. What Annette did for me in a short space of time no doctor, no therapist and no support worker could do for me in twenty years. Annette even helped me fill out an application form to volunteer on the farm.

Then, I found out I was dyslexic through Crisis. Not long after I stopped my regular psychiatrist appointments too. You would think that finding out you're dyslexic – having some answers and explanations! – would make you happy but if I'm very honest it makes me angry knowing that I had to suffer for twenty years for no reason. Even if I put myself to one side, I'm concerned about all the vulnerable people out there who have problems they don't understand and don't know how to deal with, can't defend themselves, and have to go through unnecessary suffering.

Since finding out I'm dyslexic, a lot has changed for me. I learnt that if you need to get from A to B, it can be straight forward for some people but for some people it can be difficult but it doesn't mean it's not achievable. With a few changes here and there to make things a bit easier you can get to your destination. So basically, you take that problem and you break it down. Then you break it down again and again until you can make sense of it so you can still achieve your goals. When I'm writing it's not straight forward. It's all in bits and pieces: bits of the middle, bits of the end, bits of the beginning. Then it is all joined up to create something meaningful. Look at a computer as being a tool with a million different tools on it. You pick which tools you want to learn and use. That's why it really helps to have computer knowledge because it gives me a way to understand my dyslexia.

My experience in life has taught me that anger can be turned from negative to positive and can be used to your advantage. It does feel like I'm doing all this for the wrong reasons but to make those wrong reasons right. But now that I have the answer to my problem, there is no stopping me. Although I do have a hard time reading because of my dyslexia, if I have to go to college in order to get a piece of paper so I can get my point across, then I will.

<u>Tutor Perspective: Annette Less</u>

Bulend's tutor from Crisis, said "Remarkable, determined, hardworking and brave, are all words that come to mind when describing Bulend Murad. Bulend has been attending Crisis Skylight since October 2011 and in this short time, has completely turned his life around.

Before attending classes at Crisis, Bulend's life was very different. Having suffered with issues affecting his mental health, Bulend was working very hard in therapy over the past three years. However, Bulend faced many challenges day to day and had low confidence. He found the simple things, like leaving home and going shopping, difficult as he found being in groups a challenge. He had a lack of energy, mainly due to his medication, and often slept for twelve hours a day.

Bulend was referred to Crisis through a friend he met in supported housing. He was quite shy and nervous about attending. However, he signed up to study literacy and numeracy, which were currently at a high entry level 3 level. Despite being anxious in a class setting, Bulend's attendance was fantastic – he worked hard and often asked for extra work to do outside of class. He worked extremely well in small groups and had a patient, caring and considerate working relationship with his peers. He often spent time patiently helping others in the group.

Bulend's literacy and numeracy improved dramatically and he soon achieved level 1 in both subjects. He then continued to achieve an amazing level 2. In an assignment, Bulend commented that: "I think that writing for me has been the best therapy I have ever had or done. But if I could talk the way I write, then I would be really happy. There is only one way for me and that is forward."

Bulend's enthusiasm for learning continued over 2012. He enrolled and had outstanding attendance on a range of courses at Crisis including: Museum of Me (an art and personal development course); Words for Work (learning the language used in employment) and ECDL. Through these courses Bulend has also achieved qualifications in Life and Living Skills and Employability Skills.

Despite finding some aspects of reading a challenge, Bulend has also attended the Crisis book club, where he has engaged in group discussion within a large reading group of 17–23 people. For someone who finds group settings difficult, this is a huge achievement and a real example of how Bulend has succeeded in pushing forward his own personal boundaries.

During a session in a literacy class, a task was set to research into a volunteering position and write a mock application. After discussing Bulend's love of animals, we talked about the possibility of Bulend volunteering at Spitalfield Farm. He researched the position and took time writing an application. He was shortly asked for an interview. Bulend had only been for one interview previously, but did extremely well and got an ongoing position volunteering at the farm. He now volunteers there two days a week and has been described by the farm as a "real asset."

Simultaneously, Bulend had been part of a cycling group at Homerton Hospital. His enthusiasm for cycling led him to be asked to lead the hospital's cycling group. When Bulend took over the hospital bike riding group, he got a note from the girl who he was taking over from saying:"The world is your oyster!" Bulend's determination and motivation to learn, volunteer and engage with life has meant that he is building himself a really positive future. The farm has also recently approached him to discuss the possibility of him also running a cycling group for them.

Furthermore, Bulend gave his time and energy last Christmas to volunteer with Crisis at Christmas. Despite disliking crowds, Bulend volunteered in the kitchen and enjoyed the sense of 'giving back'. He is going to volunteer again this Christmas as a Kitchen Porter.

After succeeding in completing so many courses at Crisis, Bulend and I discussed the possibility of him volunteering in an Entry Level Literacy course at Crisis. He filled in an application, did exceptionally well in the interview and now volunteers on a weekly basis as a Learning Support Volunteer. Bulend is fantastic working in the classroom. He has a great rapport with the learners and has a calm and patient manner. He has been excellent at supporting learners with spelling and reading.

Bulend modestly stated that, "I don't know why but, in the past year, everything has gone right for me." The truth is that he has shown strength and utter determination, overcome personal challenges and has truly turned his life around. He is now working hard to decrease his medication. He has grown in confidence and developed his own strategies to overcome fears and anxieties, so much so, that he is now helping so many others through his volunteering. He advises people to "not think so much but... just do" and is a true inspiration.

Crisis

Crisis is the national charity for single homeless people. Our purpose is to end homelessness. Homelessness is devastating, leaving people vulnerable and isolated. We believe everyone deserves a place to call home and the chance to live a fulfilled and active life. Lack of skills and qualifications can lead to people becoming homeless and keep them there, isolated from society, work and financial stability. Education is at the heart of Crisis – supporting people to build knowledge and skills, grow in confidence and feel more positive about the future.

Crisis Skylight London offers practical and creative workshops in an accessible and inspiring environment together with formal learning opportunities that lead to qualifications and can help people to find work. Learning to use a computer at our IT classes moves people closer to employment and financial stability, while literacy and numeracy classes help people cope better with everyday life, budgeting or paying the bills. More than 1,700 people took part in a learning activity at Crisis Skylight London last year.

Hilary Cameron, Lead Scotland

I first came out of hospital in 2001. A nurse at the hospital told me about a man who was a learner with Lead Scotland. I contacted him and he put me in touch with a learning co-ordinator with Lead Scotland based in Elgin in 2003. I got support and started off with working through computer basics and then went on to do ECDL.

A number of years later in 2012 my Key Worker from Moray Resource Centre approached me to ask if I would like to go back with Lead again. There was no question, I jumped at the chance. Since meeting Barbara Taylor, Lead Co-ordinator, I have, under her supervision, got a certificate for refreshing my skills with Access. Then I moved on to do the British Computer Society Digital Skills course – again getting a certificate.

This was a great time for me; I now had something to do. Through Lead and work I have done with them, I now have become a volunteer with the organisation, which I thoroughly enjoy. I support a learner to improve his literacy skills and computer skills.

I have gained a lot of confidence over the past two years, particularly communicating with other people. Through Moray Resource Centre I am also supporting another service user to learn more about how to use the computer and working through the Digital Skills course.

My ambition is to develop this side of my work further. I am willing to come into the Moray Resource Centre on another day to support more learners. It is a very special place for disabled people.

I am involved with the Speyside Friendship Group and make posters for their coffee mornings. I do the invitations for the Red Cross Christmas party. I surf the web, play games, and keep in touch with my friends through email – but I do not like Facebook!

In October last year, I received a Highly Commended Award in the Dr Ethel Gray Volunteer of the Year Awards run by Lead Scotland. The two learners I support nominated me and I was presented with the award by Norman MacAskill who is Lead's North Regional Development Manager.

Anyone who requires a new skill – I would say, go for it – go for it, you have nothing to lose. The more skills you have the better. This keeps the mind active, and healthy.

Lead Scotland

Lead Scotland, Linking Education and Disability, widens access to learning for marginalised disabled young people, adult learners and carers. At a local level, we provide direct support to learners through impartial guidance and support to overcome barriers and plan their learning journeys. We involve volunteer support in our service delivery and offer the loan of digital technologies. Each learner is supported to develop their own action plan and outcomes, resulting in a tailored and unique service from Lead. Many learners begin the action planning or the actual learning journey in their own home, as confidence can be one of the initial barriers to their involvement. We also have a national helpline and we influence policy and strategy to promote inclusion at a national level.

The Scottish Government's Statement of Ambition for adult learning provides a favourable policy landscape for lifewide, lifelong and learner centred learning in Scotland, being part of the programme for government. We integrate literacies skills development and digital literacy within our service models which has a good fit with the national Literacies Plan.

D, St Andrew's Birmingham

My Adult Learner Journey

My name is D and I am currently in a secure care service. From childhood, for various reasons I missed out on a stable education and so as an adult I have a lot to catch up on. I chose to study whilst in secure healthcare because I was offered the opportunity to study one to one. I took this up immediately as I have always struggled in groups.

As a child I could not concentrate but could not always get the support. I was distracted. I moved house and children's homes many times, which was unsettling and I could therefore never concentrate as I felt lost and confused. As an adult I am willing to learn and try very hard to stay focused but I still find groups difficult for many reasons.

My own achievements in very small steps inspired me to keep going. I used to see people reading the daily paper or playing scrabble on the ward. I would discuss this with my teacher and was encouraged to keep trying and build up my belief in myself. I practise reading aloud in my one to one sessions and I have learnt how to sound out unknown words by breaking them down into chunks. I have also learnt how to use clues on the page, such as headings, diagrams, labels so I can guess what the words may be from these clues.

I am very proud to say that through the Open College Network I have gained certificates in English. I worked hard and built up a portfolio of my work, which was checked by an assessor. I have so far gained: entry level 2, grammar and punctuation, reading and writing.

I am working on further units at the same level and also one at entry level 3. The options that I currently have for learning are education sessions, access to the library on-site, IT, and horticulture. The limits are mainly that I can only have one to one education one hour per week but if I were in school or college I would have whole days.

I overcame my difficulties as I matured as an adult and saw that I really wanted to learn. Encouraged by others and by my own self-motivation, I feel more positive. I like choosing what I want to study as I like certain things such as looking at world maps and talking about countries, cooking, looking at recipes and studying the words in the recipes. More recently I have found out that I really enjoy working at the allotment. It is very good for me and in my education sessions I read and write about it for my portfolio work.

My message to others who wish they had more confidence as adult learners is that if I can do it you can do it. By the way, I am now the one in the lounge playing scrabble on the ward thanks to people believing in me and most importantly thanks to believing in myself. Thanks for reading this.

Anon, St Andrew's Birmingham

My Adult Learning Journey

I have been in the psychiatric healthcare system for twenty-one years. I have at times been very unwell. As a result I have struggled with my motivation.

In the community I studied four GCSE's which included psychology, law, sociology and English, so education has always been important to me. During my time at St Andrew's and in previous settings, I have studied pet therapy and photography. Within these subjects I have created portfolios involving written text which showed my literacy skills and abilities. It was fun and motivating.

Due to being in hospital I felt that at times I missed out on study opportunities due to staff shortages. At other times, however, this was not the case and I had opportunities as hoped for. Lack of access to opportunities in the community was sometimes hard to deal with. As living with mental heath difficulties has its up and downs, it was part and parcel of my experience.

I have a lot of family support. I have had a lot of support from the education team at St Andrew's and other hospitals. Sometimes it gives you focus on what you want in life and including your aspirations. You're never too old to learn and just because you are in a psychiatric unit it does not mean you cannot study. You don't have to miss out.

I feel thankful to the Lord that he has been there for me. I missed out on college because of being in hospital and this was difficult. But you can overcome these obstacles with help.

I would like to share my story anonymously. Thank you for reading it.

Y, St Andrew's Birmingham

My Adult Learner Journey

Hello my name is Y. I am twenty-two years old and I live in the West Midlands area. I'm originally from South Wales and I am a Muslim. I went to a mainstream school where I learnt the basics in maths, English and Welsh. I really enjoyed learning Welsh. When I went to high school I started to learn the above subjects in more depth along with other subjects including science and French. I loved going to school as I got to see my friends and catch up with them.

I then went to a secure hospital where I took the opportunity to further my education in literacy and maths, achieving literacy at level 1. I did this course because I wanted to gain more qualifications in English as this was an area I needed improvement on. I have also recently enrolled on a course external to the hospital which is in British Sign Language (BSL), as this is a subject I really enjoy. Doing this studying has helped provide structure to my day and helped with my therapeutic engagement.

Due to where I was studying there were many difficulties which included: escorting to the education department, staffing levels, my own physical and mental health problems and the side effects of medication I was taking. However, there have been many people who have helped me to achieve and these people have included: teachers, technical instructors, occupational therapists and my multidisciplinary team.

My message to you is that studying education in your adult life can help give you a better chance at a more successful job in the future and, like me, it will help you in life.

St Andrew's Birmingham
St Andrew's Birmingham is a regional site of St Andrew's, an independent national teaching hospital pioneering in mental health. St Andrew's is a university learning and research centre partnered with Kings College London. It is the UK's leading charity providing specialist NHS care.

The Birmingham site consists of eight units covering three care pathways: men's mental health, women's mental health and ASD (men's). A small team offers education as part of the therapeutic programme. Many of our learners have one to one education sessions or very small groups (two to three), where we promote self–esteem by encouraging patients' motivation to take part in education sessions. We embed literacy, numeracy, and IT skills through personalised learning programmes. We work with a range of other disciplines, including occupational therapy and psychology to encourage engagement in as many different ways as possible. Our patients have complex mental health needs and issues which impact on concentration and motivation but they gain confidence over time to engage in sessions. We shared three learners' stories with you here.

Mark Nourse, HMP Winchester

My name is Mark and I was raised in London. I went to Oliver Goldsmith's primary school in Peckham, South London. My first year there in nursery was amazing. I had so much fun making new friends and playing with water and sand pits. I felt like I had arrived.

Then came the day when we had to move to the main school, Year 1 primary. I was filled with a few anxieties though most of all I remember feeling so excited. I arrived early on my first day and took my place in Mrs Clements' class. I was sitting next to a girl whose name I can't remember though who was to have such a dramatic effect on my whole learning life.

Mrs Clements asked me to draw in our book a margin. I had no idea what this word meant. So, innocently I asked my new teacher what this word was. At this, the girl sitting next to me laughed and for the first time in my life I felt ashamed, embarrassed and stupid. The class all joined in the laughter, including Mrs Clements, probably only at my innocence. My school life changed in an instant. I reacted with aggression to my shame-driven anger.

I was removed from mainstream learning and placed in the class for special children. My mind remained closed to learning for the next forty years. Rather than risk anyone thinking I was stupid, I would cover my fears with cocky disruptive behaviour. I was even too scared and embarrassed to show anyone my handwriting.

So, I am totally amazed that I am sitting here writing this story. I can only believe this is due to the confidence I have gained from Jane, who is the Employability Skills tutor attached to the carpentry course in Winchester prison.

For the first time in my life I have a thirst for the development of my self-esteem and learning new skills. Each new day my confidence grows in the knowledge that it's OK to make mistakes as long as I keep learning from them. I would encourage anyone who is held back by their fears to let go and follow their hearts.

I originally enrolled on the carpentry course because I wanted to learn how to cut a mitre joint and improve some skills with using power tools. To date I have far exceeded my expectations and now hope to push my educational boundaries to new levels every day.

I have learnt to make photo frames of different styles and finishes. I have also manufactured a television stand, bookshelf and a box with dovetail joints to hold letters. All these skills have led to me completing the Safe Use of Woodworking Machinery exams. Along with the workshop exams, I have completed numerous employability exams. These include: tools and equipment for a practical activity; occupational taster; living in a diverse society; communicate in a business environment; and Award in Employability Skills.

I have trained to become a peer mentor for Phoenix Futures and have completed their mental health awareness exam along with numerous others.

At this present time I feel very grateful to all the teachers and facilitators who have taken the time to help me to believe in myself and that the world is not such a scary place with a little formal training. "A work in progress... !

Tutor perspective: Jonathan Small

Mark came to his placement with very low self esteem and a fear of looking stupid although he did confide he wanted to improve his literacy. I agreed to provide him with extra work to complete outside of the lessons and to coach him one to one when time allowed. He has worked diligently on his spelling and his writing has improved significantly. The biggest change, however, is in his self belief and willingness to contribute to class discussion without fear of being belittled. He has encouraged his peers to benefit from education and is currently acting as a role model/mentor to a young learner.

Sabrina

I am a person who like things to be done before anybody tells me what to do.

For example: when I'm home I don't have time for myself. The first thing I do when I wake up in the morning is run in the kitchen, get breakfast ready, wake my children up and my partner's brothers because they have to go to school, feed my children, then put the cartoons on and let them watch while I clean the kitchen and put some clothes in the washing machine. Then I get my children dressed, clean my bedroom, well, all the house not only my bedroom, take the clothes out from the washing machine. By the time over again it is nearly lunch time, so I have to cook something. Then clean all over again. When I finish, I play with my children or we go in the park. When we come home, my children are tired, so they go to bed for one or two hours. When they are sleeping, I get the iron ready to iron the clothes. When my children wake up, it's already five o'clock. I have to get dinner ready, give my children a bath, put their pyjamas on, and let them watch the TV for a while, then take them to bed. I tell them a story while they fall asleep. I have a shower, watch a bit of TV and again before I get to bed, I make sure everything is clean and locked up. Then I go to bed myself.

But from now on things are going to change. When I get out from here, I want to sort things out for myself. I want to put all that energy into opening my life.

I'm going to put my children in nursery and do my courses to be an interpreter. I want my dream to come true and to be an interpreter is my dream. I want to sort my life out. I don't want to end up in prison again. I have enough of being away from children. Since I've been in prison, I realise what I've been missing and all I could've done while I was outside but I was too busy cleaning and cooking, so I never had time to think about anything else.

Tutor Perspective: Sarah Freeman
Sabrina wrote this prose poem shortly before release from a UK women's prison.

Sabrina was imprisoned for over one year, a much longer period than necessary. While she was inside, bitterly missing her two young sons, she benefited from education. She began to recognise in herself that maternal organising streak; in her case, perhaps, that had been wasted on too much home keeping before. Sabrina was clear that the chance to study English (she came to the UK as a refugee as a child with her family from Bosnia) was life-changing. She hadn't attended school in Bosnia or the UK before, and as she applied herself steadily over fourteen months, she achieved a level 1 pass in English.

D, Weston College with HMP Portland

My Life with Education

My name is D. I'm twenty-six years old. I have four children. I live in Bristol with my nan and dad and I have a beautiful girlfriend.

When I was at school, I hated it! I just found school boring. I was just not interested. I just couldn't wait to leave! I did stay at school to finish my GCSEs but had quite poor results. They were either poor or I failed them! At the age of sixteen, when I left school, I joined the army. From the first day of joining, I felt like I belonged. It was my passion! To top it all off, I didn't need any qualifications to join. I just needed to be fit. I loved it when I was in the army, loved the fitness, the chance to explore, that you always have someone looking out for you and the chance to defend my country.

I joined the army in 2005. After three tours of Iraq, I started my tours of Afghanistan. On my sixth tour of Afghanistan (2009), I was captured as a prisoner of war. I was captured for fifty eight days before we escaped. After this, I was taken off active duty because I was suffering with post traumatic stress disorder. I was still in the army though as a Recruitment Officer in Bristol. As a Recruitment Officer, it was my job to go around to year assemblies to inspire the young adults to join the army when they finish school. After doing this for three years, I received an honourable discharge from the army.

In 2013 I ended up stealing petrol as I couldn't afford to keep taking my disabled son to hospital, which was a two hundred mile round trip every day. As a consequence, I ended up coming to prison!!! After being in prison for six months, I decided that when I was released from prison, I wanted to go to college to study auto electrics. As education was free while I was in prison and I had time on my hands, I decided to take level 2 in maths and English, as well as lots of level 2 courses in other subjects, so I could start on level 2 in auto electrics instead of starting on level 1. When I started doing education again, I was surprised to find that I really enjoyed it.

When I decided to start education again, I found I had to overcome some things. I was at a lower level than what I thought I was and what I needed. I had to study harder than everyone in my class. I had to learn more than everyone but I only had the same time as everyone else. I needed to be highly motivated! I did have some blocks to overcome as well, like dyslexia. I found it hard to read anything that wasn't on a blue background. It was hard to complete work on time. I really had to work hard! The way I overcame my blocks was PURE DETERMINATION. I was determined to pass level 2 maths and English, so I got my head down and studied.

I'm now an English peer mentor. I help students who are in a similar situation as I was in with their English studies. I help them to learn and be ready for their exams. It's a trusted position as I help the teacher with administration forms and I also do important administration work. I honestly believe education has changed my life. It has given me things to work towards and new goals in life. When I'm released from prison, it's going to give me the chance to start on level 2 auto electrics instead of level 1. It has also given me the confidence to help my children with their homework, instead of looking for an excuse not to!

All I can say to anyone who feels lost or who is not sure what to do with their lives, is to think about education. It can open doors, give you confidence, and you're never too old to learn. It also might save your life like it did mine. I am now twenty-six years old. I used to hate education but now I very much enjoy it. After my time in the army, I thought my life was over. To be honest, with the help of education, I now realise my life is just starting over!

J L, Weston College with HMP Leyhill

J L's Inspirational Story

My name is J and I have Asperger's. I am a family man and I am happiest when I am at home. I have two boys aged eight and nine years old. I have had no formal education. When I was at primary school, I used to continually press the fire alarms as I liked the fire engines coming to the school. I was asked to leave at twelve years old. I therefore have no formal education or certifications. When I was clinically diagnosed with autism, the psychiatrist stated that I would never achieve any qualifications; I would never progress above an entry 1 qualification.

I started my education at forty-four years old in prison. I took this path as I thought there is more to life than crime and I want to be at home to support my sons with their homework. I want to improve my English and maths for everyday life. I want to be able to read and understand everyday forms, like application forms. I want to be able to read and understand rules so that it will bring my anxiety down. It will give me a better quality of life.

I have lots of challenges in regards to education. If I could identify my biggest obstacle, it would be smells.

Certain smells trigger certain memories, so it can make me feel very anxious. They changed the cleaning materials used in education ,which reminded me of a hospital, so that made me very anxious. Smells have a very big effect on how I feel. There aren't any wheels, or anything with circular movement in education, so that isn't very good. It was difficult to meet new teachers and hard to accept that a favourite teacher, Debbie, had left. It is a busy department and that made me feel very anxious. I had to force myself to come through the door. Underlying all of this is the ultimate fear of failure.

If it wasn't for my teacher, Chloe, and the education manager, Dan, I would have not entered the education building. They understand me. They have encouraged me to keep going when I have wanted to give up. They have changed the teaching, so that I can receive one to one support and teaching. They made learning enjoyable for the first time ever!

I have completed an entry 3 Functional Skills qualification in English. This consists of three components: reading, writing and speaking and listening. This is two grades higher than what the psychiatrists initially said I was capable of achieving. I am also studying maths at Level 1. I currently work in reception. My duties include escorting people to their rooms with their belongings, filling out property cards, logging down valuables, box numbers and prisoner numbers. I wouldn't have been able to do these tasks before I started education. I wouldn't have been able to fill in the forms correctly before I learnt this in English. Education also gave me the confidence to talk to new people, as we practiced this in education as part of the speaking and listening exam. I have visited the library for the first time ever. I would have never achieved the confidence to walk through the library doors. I now enjoy reading. I can get knowledge and it helps your brain. Before, I never really understood why people read. I also write letters home, something I have never done before. My progression has since resulted in my psychiatrist re-assessing me and re diagnosing me with high functioning Asperger's. I was initially diagnosed with low functioning Asperger's.

It is going to help me help my sons, in particular Jack. I have now changed my view on schools and understand that it is a good thing for Jack to get a good education. I can now help Jack with his homework and feel confident to go into his school. I will also go into Jimmy's school and support him with his educational journey. I won't be so anxious when I have to fill in a form at the doctors or bank. I now have these skills, so I won't feel so anxious.

I would say to others who are reluctant to engage in education to come and see Chloe and Dan. It isn't as scary as you think! Education can open up a lot of avenues and make you feel more confident. You should always try it and see how it goes. For people like me, first impressions are crucial. The first meeting has to go well. From then things can go better.

Weston College with HMP Services

Weston College deliver learning and skills to thousands of offenders in prisons across the South West, and immigration centres. The teams focus on providing outstanding delivery to learners, to help them with their learning and raising aspirations whilst also ensuring that the education provided meets the needs of the learners and employers.

Chris Nicholls, Buckinghamshire Adult Learning

The first time I sat in the training room I couldn't say anything. By the second workshop I felt able to ask some questions. Now, I don't shut up. Since completing the course and winning the award (Festival of Learning), I've done assemblies in front of five hundred people. I've done radio, spoken at the awards ceremony and spoken to the training team at Buckinghamshire Adult Learning. I couldn't have done it without Alan.

It was both of us who did it. We worked together. He believed in me and had so much patience. I remember him sitting with me explaining what the questions on the mock exam meant, explaining it to me. Once I understood what they were asking me to do, I found it so much clearer and I could do it. He changed my life for the better. I've got belief in myself. I finally believe I'm not stupid.

The learning I did has changed family life as well as work. Big changes. I've got a purpose. I think I can do things now. I don't let people tell me I can't do things because I've done it – I've already achieved! Now I want to keep doing it and achieve more. I want to keep on learning.

I'm not just a number any more; now I'm someone who counts. People come to me to ask me things. Children at school come to see me and there's respect there. I now help them out with reading, which for someone like me with dyslexia is such a good feeling. I want to help them like Alan helped me.

I can't forget the day I got my award. Apart from my children being born, it was one of the most special days of my life.

The difference for me is the confidence it gives you. You can show people that no matter how stupid you think you are, you can learn and you can achieve.

I don't just want to be a caretaker any more. I want to do more. Onwards and upwards!

Tutor Perspective: Alan Hester

I need to say to begin with that I am not a literacy tutor! I was Chris's tutor for a management qualification that he completed last year. As the course was funded through an adult apprenticeship route, it included English, maths and ICT Functional Skills; all of which had to be achieved if Chris were to achieve his framework qualification.

I had already worked with him to achieve a Team Leading NVQ two years previously, during which time he told me that he was dyslexic and had not achieved at school as a result. Therefore when he and his employers applied for the higher level, I explained that he would need to do some English tests. His response was that if I would help him then he would do whatever was necessary in order to pass them. With that attitude, I was more than happy to agree to help.

I can honestly say that working with Chris and seeing the transformation in him has been a highlight of my current role. Chris has been generous in his praise for my part in his success, but it couldn't have happened without his attitude and commitment.

Chris clearly loves learning. He has taken so much on board during the programme, in particular listening and communication skills, and is proving himself to be a very good people manager. In the process he has tackled English, maths and ICT with the same determination and, I have to say, pleasure. He's right when he says that we worked together, and in the process I've also learnt from him. Every trainer loves to find that 'breakthrough' moment for a learner, and he was an obvious choice for me to recommend for an Adult Learner of the Year Award (now Festival of Learning).

Gillian Lawrence, Up Your Street

"Up Your Street is a free online sharing service highlighting activities and events for seniors around the Queen Elizabeth Olympic Park."

I actively encouraged and motivated three senior women, of average age seventy, to follow a two year course in Visual Art Appreciation. There was Pratibha, Su Wong and Daphne. We all went along to the introductory session in a community art centre in West Ham, east London and the course was directed by a well-established British university in West London.

Su Wong was extremely nervous and refused to sign on the dotted line. She confided in me, "I am scared of failing." She went away. Now as far as I know, these are women who finished formal education a long time ago. Daphne asked me, "What is research?"

I badgered Su, "You will get help. This is a course where you will learn loads and how will your grandchildren be proud of you just for thinking about it? And for you, Su? You can do it." Meanwhile my friend was telling Daphne, "You can do this. You can."

Pratibha had already signed all the papers and bought some new pens and folders.

The three women went together each Tuesday to West Ham and I never saw Pratibha and Daphne for a whole year. I continued to leave messages to let them know I was interested in how they were getting along. At last we all arranged to meet at The Tate Britain for an event about art and debates. We caught up and I heard stories of nightmare essays, and spending time in museums of art and flows about visual appreciation and how some artists they now know very well and that there's art everywhere and look at that architecture. Su had fallen in love with Doric columns.

I was already proud of the three women after the first year. I was proud that they persevered at it all and chummied along together. They had to travel into central London most evenings in the winter for university lectures. I invited Daphne, who was passionate about The Nehru Gallery at The Victoria and Albert Museum, London, to do a self-led tour of the exhibition with a group from Up Your Street. She was amazing: She had her notes and her wonderful stòry-telling ways. In asides, she'd ask me if she were doing okay. All I saw was confidence and her great love of ancient art.

Su was gradually withdrawing. Her emails to me were infrequent. She was incredibly busy with collecting her grandchild from school every day. I could not help but reminded myself that all we women are seniors and have succeeded over many hurdles. I could not worry for her. Pratibha announced that she'd won learner of the year award but hated being in the spotlight, so I had to keep her glory close to my heart and glee. Daphne refused to respond to my emails and texts. Her head was in a tunnel.

Another year passed and the results were out but secret from me. The three had become a two and a one. Su and Daphne finally confessed to me on a bus journey that they had failed... by two points. I saw two lifeless depressed women who had nowhere to turn. Su became ill and went into hospital. I phoned the tutor and told her about the doldrums. She emphasised how retakes were possible. Four months later Pratibha told me she'd passed and gone to another level.

In August 2015 Daphne sent up her last essay. No-one was sure whether Su was working on essays or not. The group of three was defunct. Su wasn't studying. We joined a women's art group and Su, in front of an audience of thirty, gave a glorious appreciation of a classical work. I was happy that her self-esteem was not dented. She went home to make raspberry jam and crochet squares for abuse survivors. Daphne has started texting again. Pratibha goes alone to any free art exhibitions.

Radha Virahsawmi, Birkbeck University

When I retired I decided to join a class to learn something constructive and worthwhile which I would enjoy, although I have not engaged in any formal course for over thirty years. I joined adult learning to study at Birkbeck University London.

The only course made available that I know at the time was Visual Art. This would involve several visits to art galleries and museums. As I am hopeless at drawing and painting, this seemed great and I joined in October 2002, studying on a part-time basis.

As a visual art student I will have to be able to describe the composition of the painting, the brushstroke used by the artist, and the use of colours, space and light to create the visual effects required. To gain better understanding of the concept, while attending classes, I made time to visit museums during my spare time, spent hours looking at art works and attended several sessions organised by the museum to give an insight about selected paintings.

The course was hard going as most of the work had to be done in my spare time. I had to make time for recommended reading for the classes as well as searching for added information. It involved attending art galleries and museums. I had to learn the use of a computer from scratch, as I had no previous knowledge of doing research for the subject. I had to learn PowerPoint, for presentation to the class, for the course work. I attended English academic workshops to better my written language and essay writing. The hardest part was remembering, especially at my age, where I tend to forget easily. It was difficult to learn and remember new words such as art vocabularies, name of art painting and the year it was painted together with the name of the artist who completed the art work, and for which I had to devise my own methods by using flip cards and regular revision. The other difficulty I had was when writing an essay. I found it difficult to present my argument. A few times I did not understand the essay question. After I completed the essay, I realised that I did not answer the question. I then had to take extra time to do further reading and rewrote the whole essay. This caused me to hand in my essay late which led to my marks being capped, causing some disappointments.

I read slower than most people and it took me a few times to understand and make reason of my readings. This I overcame by spending more time and reading only a few pages at a time, more than a couple of times. Studying had an impact on my social life; then again I selected only the ones that interested me the most. As for family life, I still did a substantial amount. My three grandchildren are grown up. They did not need me for babysitting anymore, so I had more spare time for my study.

It has been a great experience, very challenging, after all very rewarding. I have achieved this through much hard work and putting in extra time. I had not taken unseen written examination for many years. Fortunately, I managed to pass which allowed me to continue for a further year. This was a great incentive.

Studying for two years at Higher Education level has increased my knowledge in visual art as well as understanding the composition of art. I intend to visit Florence again but this time I will look at paintings, architecture and statues with a better understanding and a different eye.

I would sincerely advise and encourage any mature person to take up some type of academic studies. Although difficult at the beginning, as the study progresses, it makes more sense and becomes clearer. What have you got to lose? Why not use up your time, to challenge yourself, by doing something rewarding? I believe that it has improved my memory and has made a major difference to the way I use my spare time.

I must add that studying at Birkbeck is the best, as all the lecturers are very approachable, understanding and a great deal of help is available from the university. I hope I have shown that it is possible for everyone to make a start at studying and I hope that many adults will join a class. You will be satisfied and will feel greatly rewarded.

Tutor Perspective: Sarah Potter

Radha Virahsawmy enrolled on the Birkbeck Certificate of Higher Education in Understanding the Visual Arts in October 2012, and is currently completing the second year. She had never studied at Level 4 before, did not know how to log on to a computer, had no knowledge of the arts, and had only rarely visited a museum. She seized the opportunity to embark on positive learning rather than continue with activities which were mainly social and got her out of the house.

Faced with the learning demands of her course, she sought help from the student support team at Birkbeck's Stratford campus. With her determination, dedication and willingness to come to the campus at weekends and in the evenings, Radha is simply an inspiration, especially in the way she has persevered and achieved with IT. She has learnt how to use Google Scholar and Google Books for her assignments. When she started, she had never heard of Google, but now uses it constantly. She has also created two fantastic PowerPoint about artists, searching for information and images on the Internet, and learning to copy, paste and move items around, resulting in two presentations that both members of her class and tutors enjoyed and praised. She was rightly proud of this achievement. She has made full use of the expertise of our library learning support advisers as well as IT technical support and an IT course in acquiring her computer skills. Our IT technicians are very impressed by the way she made progress. Her family have benefited too, since she now emails her three grandsons, and also her relatives in India, using her newly acquired laptop.

Radha has attended study skills workshops to improve her academic reading and writing, and with one to one help has learnt to organise her essays and develop an argument. She has learnt how to conduct her own research for her assignments by developing Information Literacy skills, working long hours with our library learning support advisers. At the same time, she has learnt to take academic criticism and respond with appropriate improvements to her work.

The outcomes of Radha's return to study have been that her tutor for her first year certificate module noted her excellent attendance (12 out of 13 classes), her submission of assignments on time, her informed contributions to class discussion always made in a pleasant way, and the clear progression in her academic grades, from 55% for the first assignment (a critical analysis), to 62% for the final assignment (a presentation). What impressed her tutor most about Radha was her determination to succeed in a new and challenging task, and the consistent way in which she put so much hard work and time into acquiring knowledge of art history and academic skills. Her tutor fully supported a nomination for an adult learner award.

In her spare time, Radha has become a frequent visitor to museums and major galleries, and is becoming more confident about her art knowledge. She still doubts herself, but always cheerfully perseveres in the face of all the pressures, and is considering progressing from her certificate onto a degree.

Radha embarked on her Understanding Visual Arts Certificate at the age of seventy, having retired at sixty-seven from working very long hours as a Housing Benefit Officer. Her husband died when he was thirty-two, and Radha was left on her own and worked to support her daughter. She has fourteen years' experience as a foster mother. It is truly impressive that she should wish to engage so wholeheartedly with the discipline of academic study and the acquisition of academic skills after a long and hard working life.

D, Learning for the Fourth Age

D was referred for support after a diagnosis of early dementia. She lived on her own and had been an artist. The brief was to find a volunteer to enable her to continue enjoying her hobby and give her purpose and distraction during the day. The care co-ordinator, Clare Miles, visited and was able to hear all about the things she enjoyed doing and see some of her paintings, as well as to talk to her son, who was D's main carer. They were able to talk about the other groups and help that was already being accessed to ensure that this was complimented and not replicated or clashed with.

The situation at home was assessed in terms of how a volunteer would enter, keep safe, inform the family and other carers of the visit, and any problems could be reported. A communication book calendar was set up to make this easier and to give D a reference and reminder for who would visit when. A volunteer was sought who would be able to cope with these different challenges and understand D's condition.

Working with D has been a hugely moving experience as her passion and progress have grown and developed despite her health setbacks. D did not remember who was visiting each week but quickly associated them with painting. D re-found all her old painting equipment over a number of weeks with help from her family. Having not painted for a while, D really enjoyed talking about her art, remembering the jobs she had had, recalling paintings and holidays, discussing styles and materials and even finishing off unfinished paintings.

After just five weekly sessions, D fell and consequently ended up in hospital and was then moved into a care home. Her box of paints and art materials went with her and we simply continued the sessions in the home. D is very comfortable painting once started on a picture and after 6–7 sessions was keen to carry on without support at the end of the session, so we left her painting things out and she enjoyed demonstrating and talking to staff and residents about what she was doing.

Being able to bring this kind of continuity of a completely individualised provision to D in the care home setting has meant that staff and residents have really got to know D and to see what she is capable of! She is not just an elderly lady with dementia; she has skill, she has passion for her interests and she has opinions and likes and dislikes she can share and demonstrate.

D has recently had a stroke and despite this we are able to keep the continuity of visits in hospital (where appropriate). We were able to bring our existing knowledge of what she enjoys to new sessions planned around her current condition and hopefully enable her to continue enjoying art.

H, Learning for the Fourth Age

H is a gentleman who referred himself to us with a very specific need. H was recently bereaved and had found himself dependent on family to do his shopping for him, which he was not happy about. He has poor mobility and lives on the second floor of managed retirement apartments. Again a home assessment visit was made to find out that H was a retired headmaster with experience of coordinating a business providing one-to-one language learning for foreign government workers.

H had a laptop but did not know how to use it. He wanted to be able to use this to communicate via email with friends and family. He also wanted to be able to do online shopping so that he was independent as much as possible and not reliant on other people to do his shopping for him. He was also clear that he wanted to be able to shop for whatever he wanted – not always what others thought he needed!

H worked with the Domiciliary Coordinator, and then with a volunteer, over the space of approximately six months. Over this time, he gained increasing confidence with the computer: with email and then the internet and with shopping online. By the end, he was independent with all of this – able to order groceries, books, presents for loved ones, search for interests and even start getting to grips with social media and blogs. H has also been able to use the internet to research and, for example, learned he was to receive some medals that had been recently awarded to all members of the Arctic Convoys during WW2.

This knowledge has given H a new lease of life and independence. He has found that he is now able to keep in touch with family and friends, do his shopping etc. He has been given a voice and social network online and has made a firm, intergenerational, friend with the volunteer, who is able to continue supporting him occasionally – even via Skype.

In this case, the key observation to make for the success was the very specific skill matching of the volunteer (an IT lecturer at the university) to the learning required and a knowledge of the person we were providing the learning to. The volunteer gave weekly or session feedback regarding the progress made, the problems encountered and any challenges set so we have a record of the work done.

Regular evaluation visits were also carried out every five to six sessions to ensure that the brief was being fulfilled. The sessions received 100 out of 100 for effectiveness, value for money and the quality of the volunteer from H!

J, Learning for the Fourth Age

J lives at home near her daughter, who works full time. J has MS and early signs of dementia. J was a musician, piano player and teacher of music. On assessment J's daughter attended and was able to prompt J to tell me all about her career in music. At home, she has all her scores and two pianos – upright and baby grand.

J was prompted by her daughter, who encouraged her to play some pieces for me. She is a very accomplished musician but J's daughter said that unless prompted she no longer plays or remembers to play and is often bored and listless at home. She is alone in the day and so the volunteer found would need to come and encourage J to play, accompany her and ask for tips and advice to give J the sense of being at work and useful.

This was a really specific challenge. Not only did the volunteer need to be an accomplished musician, but also to understand the health issues, the possible effects on J and the challenges they could present. It took us a while until a suitable volunteer was placed – a professional musician, teacher of violin but also learning piano herself. She has an interest in the effect of music on the brain, the therapeutic benefits of playing or listening to music and personal experience of caring for an older relative. She has developed a good relationship with the family and with J and they are able to play together and to challenge each other with new pieces and old favourites.

The family have now seen J playing and enjoying her music again and they always have something to listen to and to ask her about. J seems to respond very positively to the sessions now – although this took some months as the routine and volunteer needed to become familiar.

"Mum likes to rehearse and is enjoying her sessions. She really responds to helping improve performance skills. It is physically and mentally demanding for her now but hopefully it's a very largely good tiredness. Mum's MS with its extra consequences, although pretty stable, has its good days and bad days. Fiona's visits have been a positive reminder of her talents and passion."

Working with J there are special considerations due to her inconsistent mobility. The volunteer needed to be able to understand her boundaries in terms of what she could and couldn't manage and work around these. The volunteer reports after each session regarding the learning achieved, health and well-being of J and any challenges faced. This enables the domiciliary coordinator to ensure that appropriate support is offered and the family informed of any problems.

This is an ongoing very positive partnership with both the volunteer and learner developing and growing in their skill and passion for music together.

<u>Tutor Perspective: Clare Miles</u>
Clare is a domiciliary care co-ordinator in the community with Learning for the Fourth Age who is sharing some anonymised life long learning case studies. As well as developing and maintaining basic literacies, these stories

demonstrate the high therapeutic and practical value of drawing on sophisticated, creative applied literacies skills acquired over the life course to maintain quality of life while in supported living.

Olivia Watkins

My name is Olivia Watkins and I am twenty-three years old and I have Down syndrome. I have two sisters and a brother. Hannah is twenty-seven; George is twenty-five, then me, then Alice who will be twenty-one in December.

I live in a flat by myself during the week, and I have two jobs. One is a voluntary job at my mum's school, in the kitchens. I have done this for two years now, and I love it. My Kitchen Manager, Celia, gives me lots of jobs to do, like cutting up fruit for Fruit Cups, icing sponges and preparing salads. My other job is a Kitchen Assistant at the University West of England. This is a paid job. My dad saw an advert in the paper and my mum helped me to fill in the application form. I had to go for an interview and I got the job. It's a very busy kitchen. There are loads of people and I work hard when I am there. Matt is my manager in this job. To get to my jobs I travel independently on a bus. On the weekend, I stay with mum and dad. We go shopping on Sunday mornings and I take my own trolley round the supermarket and get everything I need for the week. Then I go to the till and pay for it all.

I went to New Siblands Special School in Thornbury when I was five. I left when I was eighteen. Then I went to Foxes Academy in Minehead, for three years. I wanted to go to Foxes because I love food and cooking and I wanted to learn new things, to live independently and to get a job. I got an NVQ Level 1 qualification for Food Preparation at Foxes, and lots more certificates for all my other learning.

When I left in 2013, I won the Outstanding Learner of the Year Award (now Festival of Learning) at Graduation Day. I was so proud and happy. Then, in 2014 I won another award. I was a Regional Award Winner for everything I had done since leaving Foxes, and I went on The Pier at Weston-Super-Mare to a lovely dinner to collect my award. I got a £200 voucher, to do some more learning, and I decided to go on a photography course, because I love taking photos, especially sunsets.

A long time before I went to Foxes, my teacher at school sent a video home, about Foxes Academy, for me to watch with mum and dad. I really liked it and decided I wanted to go there when I left school. It took a long time to get my place, but I was very happy and excited when I found out I would be going. I went to look at some other colleges, but I didn't like them as much as Foxes Academy. If I went to a college near home, I wouldn't have learnt so much about being a chef, and living independently, which is what I wanted to do. Foxes taught me how to travel independently and safely too. I am really good at using the bus now.

In my learning, I had to work very hard, and pay attention and follow instructions. Sometimes I found this hard, but not often. I worked in the Foxes Hotel during the day and lived in a house with other learners afterwards. I never lived with strangers before, or lived away from home for a long time. I was very nervous at the start of Year 1, and I missed my family, but I got on with it and then I made new friends, and really enjoyed it. It took me a little while to learn what to do, but the staff were brilliant, and helped me if I had any problems. At Foxes I did House-Keeping, Food Service and Food Preparation. I also had "Moving On" sessions every week. This helped me improve my reading, writing, maths and IT skills, so that when I left I could get a job, and be able to manage money and live independently. I took English speaking board qualifications to help me with my speech. I learned how to read bus timetables and recipes. I wrote weekly shopping lists and went to the shops to buy things, using my money. I learned how to use the cashpoint at the bank to get money out, when I needed it.

When I was at Foxes, I kept thinking about what I wanted to do when I finished my course. I kept telling myself to work hard and I knew I could do it. I worked in a real hotel kitchen, which was really busy sometimes. But, I knew that staff were always there to help me if I got stuck or didn't understand. There were lots of signs and symbols, words and pictures around to help me too. The other learners were my friends and we all helped each other. We had a great time.

Going to college at Foxes gave me the skills I needed to get on with my life. My mum and dad and my family are very happy with me because I worked very hard to get my targets – a job and living independently. I don't think I could have done this if I hadn't gone to college, and I don't know what I would be doing with my life now. Because I went to Foxes and got my qualifications, I got my two jobs and my flat. I have loads of friends and I do loads of socialising. Whenever I am out, I always meet someone I know. I have made friends in my jobs too. I am really happy with my life actually.

If I had friends that were talking about going to college now, I would tell them to definitely go. Go for it! You will learn so much, and if you try really hard, you can get a job, a paid job, like me and then, if you want, you can live independently. I would tell them not to worry, because there will be staff to help you and you will have a great time. You have to get on with your life – like me!

Parental Perspective: Lynne Watkins

My name is Lynne Watkins and I am Olivia Watkin's mum! Olivia has Down Syndrome and associated learning difficulties. She is twenty three years of age at present. From a very young age, Olivia has been a determined young lady, a real character, always wanting to learn and achieve and have great fun along the way! There were challenges of course, but firm boundaries, high expectations and a lot of patience from a lot of people have shaped the amazing Olivia we all know and love today.

Olivia attended a local special school from the ages of five to eighteen years, where the expertise, patience and dedication of the staff enabled her to thrive, physically, emotionally and academically. In turn, Olivia was able to make the huge transition from school to a residential college, seventy miles away from home, at the age of eighteen. Olivia left school being able to read and write well. Her grasp of numeracy skills were ok, and we knew that she would have to improve and develop these skills to enable her to fulfil her potential, and her goal, "To get on with my life!"

Around the age of fourteen to fifteen years, Olivia expressed a continued wish that when she finished school, she would like to go to Foxes Academy. Olivia had watched a documentary about Foxes and clearly thought it was the place to be!

Whilst Olivia worked hard at school, and enjoyed much fun, my husband Ray and I worked very hard to ensure that she had the best possible opportunities available to her on leaving school. The local authority's view and desire was that Olivia should attend a local college provision. Ray and I, with and without Olivia, visited numerous local colleges. We were very open-minded and tried to find what Olivia was looking for within them. Sadly, we were unable to find anything on offer locally that would have met Olivia's needs and, and perhaps more importantly, her aspirations. There was nothing to match what Foxes had to offer.

Ray and I put a case forward to the local authority, detailing our findings, and confirming what we had known all along - Foxes Academy was the way forward and provided everything that would meet Olivia's needs, develop her skills further, and enable her to take her place in society. Olivia told family and friends that she wanted a job and to live independently when she had finished college. Ray and I were determined to provide her with the very best opportunities to realise these goals.

Having put our case together, the wait for a decision began. We had been advised that we may not receive a decision until late summer holidays 2010. However, we received the news that funding for the full three year course had been agreed in May 2010!

From September 2010 to July 2013, Olivia attended Foxes Academy in Minehead, Somerset. Here she received a personalised learning experience, tailored to her developmental and academic needs and requirements. During the course, Olivia developed the skills to live independently and to seek employment when she left. Foxes delivered a "Moving On" course to its students, which developed Olivia's literacy and numeracy skills still further. Olivia learnt how to follow recipes, to weigh ingredients, to follow health and safety guidance. All of the foundations laid at school were built on, developed and consolidated at Foxes. Olivia learnt vital life skills relating to her personal safety, money and how to use and save it. She learnt how to compile a shopping list, how to use that list in a shop, and how to pay for her goods. Her IT skills were improved and she has an excellent grasp of iPod and iPad now, teaching me a thing or too along the way!

To enable her to travel, Olivia undertook travel training, using public transport, initially with a buddy, and then independently. She continues to use the bus, travelling to and from work. She can read a bus time table and use a clock to determine what time she needs to be ready by.

When Olivia graduated from Foxes Academy, she won The Outstanding Learner of the Year Award (now Festival of Learning). She was delighted and inspired even further to get a job, live independently and, as she repeatedly told us, "get on with my life!"

Olivia now has two jobs. She works voluntarily, two days a week as a Kitchen Assistant in a primary school, and two days a week in a paid job, as a Kitchen Assistant at The University West of England. She lives in a one-bedroomed flat, by herself and enjoys an enviable social life! She catches the bus to and from work, and sometimes to visit us!

Olivia also belongs to The Firebird Theatre Company, based at The Bristol Old Vic Theatre. Here, she has to read and follow a script, listen to instructions and work collaboratively with the Firebirds team. In November she will participate in "Prospero, Duke of Milan" from Shakespeare's The Tempest, which The Firebirds will perform.

In May 2014, Olivia won a Regional Adult Learner's Week Award (now Festival of Learning), and attended a grand dinner on The Pier at Weston-super-Mare. With her award money, Olivia decided to go on a photography course to develop her knowledge and skills in this area.

Olivia considers herself to be a life-long learner, and Ray and I see that in the way she approaches life. She is happy, confident and driven to achieve her goals and be the best that she can be. Her family, friends and work colleagues are very proud of her, and she is treasured!

Foxes Academy

"a hospitality and training hotel for young adults with learning disabilities"

Olivia joined Foxes Academy in September 2010 for a three year programme. She has Down syndrome with associated significant learning disabilities. She has communication difficulties and physical difficulties and wears orthotic inserts to help maintain her foot alignment. The following is an excerpt from her ILP from September 2010 which shows her starting point: "I am progressing towards speaking without relying on Makaton. I am vulnerable in the community and I need help to spot dangers. I need support to understand stranger danger and reminding not to speak to people I do not know. I can be easily led, this makes me vulnerable. I can get angry and frustrated when I can't do something. I can appear confident but I need help to complete familiar tasks without becoming anxious and losing focus. I need support to interact with my friends. I need support to access the community and reminders of personal safety. I need support to interact with my friends. I need guidance and encouragement to complete tasks." The following comments describe Olivia's incredible learning journey, how she faced these challenges, overcame her learning barriers and transformed her life so that she now lives in supported living accommodation and has not one but two jobs!

Employability and Personal Development: Olivia shows a very keen interest in cooking and food prep and has shown a real determination to learn the skills to enable her to fulfil her long term goal to find paid work after leaving Foxes Academy. She has made exceptional progress and achieved the following: level 1 in food preparation and cooking (2012), an Award in Employability and Personal Development at entry level 2 in 2012 and an entry level 3 certificate in 2013. She also gained level 1 in food safety (2013). Olivia completed a very successful thirteen week work placement in a local care home who would have offered her employment if she stayed in the area.

Independent Living Skills: Initially Olivia was quiet and often in the background looking to others to speak for her. Well that was then and this is now. Oh my, what a difference. She has made incredible progress right across the board with all daily living skills. Right from the start she was determined to succeed and this attitude has enabled her to achieve many personal goals as well as course targets. The more she has learnt, the more confidence she has gained, particularly in Personal Hygiene, Personal Awareness, Social Skills and Community Access. Olivia has further developed her community skills by regularly using the bus. She can now use the internet to find the bus timetable and is able to work out a suitable time to leave and a time of return. Olivia has shown great focus and tenacity and this is testament to her determination to succeed and be the best she can. Olivia gained an Award (entry level 2) in Personal and Social Development in 2013. She also gained English Speaking Board qualifications starting a pre-entry level in 2010, entry level 2 (with Certificate of Excellence) in 2011 and entry level 3 in 2013, which is incredible considering she used to rely on Makaton for communicating.

Skills for Life: Olivia has put 100% into improving her literacy, numeracy and ICT skills. She gained City and Guilds entry level 1 in numeracy in 2011 and then went on to achieve an entry level 2 in 2012. She gained an entry level 2 in literacy in 2011 and an entry level 3 in 2012. She also gained an entry level 2 qualification in ICT.

The following is a letter from Olivia's mother which clearly states the positive impact on her life: "Olivia is working voluntarily, two days a week at Wheatfield Primary School, in the kitchen, and loving it. There are 410 pupils, so it is a really busy kitchen environment but she is doing very well. Olivia travels by bus to work and was adamant that she didn't want a "C" on her bus pass, saying that she caught the bus whilst at Foxes and she is an independent traveller, she doesn't need a Companion! I couldn't argue with that could I?" She had an interview for a job at the University of the West of England as a General Kitchen Assistant. Olivia filled in the application form herself and was delighted when the letter came inviting her for an interview. Olivia has been offered two days paid employment at UWE.

In terms of housing, Olivia moved into a supported living home at the end of September with her friend for a three month trial but this did not work out through no fault of Olivia's. We are all incredibly proud of her achievements. She has grown in maturity and confidence. Also over this time she has found her own voice and has grown into a popular and increasingly independent young lady. Olivia is articulate, determined, motivated and hard working. Olivia says, "I am really proud of what I have achieved since being at Foxes. I have learnt how to do loads of things. I am especially proud of myself because I am now taking responsibility for all my daily routines and jobs".

Foxes are so proud of Olivia's achievements and undeterred by the challenges her disability poses. She is proving to be a huge inspiration to others.

Susannah Chambers

A Learner's Story of Resilience – A Tutor's Perspective

Learners' stories of resilience do not always have to be high-profile and dramatic. Indeed, during my time working as an adult learning tutor and having worked with hundreds of learners over the years, one story of resilience stands out above the rest. It was exceptional in its ordinariness. Awe-striking in its simplicity. Moving in the ever-presence for that learner of the underlying cause for difficulty.

The learner – who, for the purposes of me re-telling this story we will call Sylvia (not her real name) – had enrolled on an adult learning programme in gardening with embedded basic skills, which I was tutoring. Sylvia committed to engaging in this course as a progression from a taster session I had delivered in her local village. She had fed back that she had really enjoyed the taster session and seemed highly motivated to progress into further learning. She had two young children and was keen to model lifelong learning to them and to develop her skills as part of preparation to return to work, she explained during her induction.

As enrolment on this course was immediately following Sylvia completing the taster session, there were no issues that presented themselves to me as a tutor through screening and initial assessment, both of which were carried out in a non-threatening and context-appropriate way. All seemed to be progressing well.

We had checked in the initial discussion at the point of enrolment that she knew where the local learning centre was and that she felt confident navigating to the college of Further Education's outreach learning centre.

The origins of Sylvia's story of resilience began in a compelling way the day that we had agreed for her to attend her first one-to-one session at the local learning centre. I arrived, as usual, in good time to ensure the classroom was comfortable and that all resources were available. The session was due to start at 2.30pm.

The clock showed 2pm. No Sylvia.

The clock showed 2.30pm. No Sylvia.

The clock showed 2.45pm. No Sylvia. And so it went on.

Concerned about her, I telephoned her.

"Hello?" Sylvia answered her mobile phone. "Oh, is it that time already? Yes, I'll definitely see you at 2pm next week. See you then!"

The following week the same occurred. And the week after. I asked Sylvia on the phone whether another day or time would be helpful. Sylvia said the day and time were fine, that she just lost track of time. And then it dawned on me that perhaps Sylvia couldn't tell the time. But that surely couldn't be the case? After all she got her kids sorted out for school, so she must have a routine? And then it dawned on me that each time I'd spoken to Sylvia she had been so keen to tell me about her favourite TV soap opera, Neighbours.

"I wonder," I thought.

So before we finished our phone call I decided to be bold and said, "Sylvia, next week, it would be great if you could come to the learning centre as soon as you finish watching Neighbours."

"Oh, OK, yeah – see you next week."

That next week I sat waiting at the learning centre fully expecting to need to make another follow-up call to discuss alternative progression routes and support needs. Suddenly, Sylvia appeared. Every week after that Sylvia was on time for class and was relaxed and ready to learn.

It transpired - as I built up a positive rapport with her during her course - that actually she had never learnt to tell the time and her whole daily routines were reliant on her children telling her the time or cues from what other family members were doing. During the course one of the skills she acquired was telling the time and by the end of the course she didn't rely on the Neighbours theme tune any more to get to class on time!

This was an important life lesson for me as a tutor that every learner, by the time they show up for that first learning experience with you, has often already built a very personal and unique life story of resilience – surviving in spite of lacking some key life skills that most around them don't give a second thought to. To empower a learner to tell that story of resilience through supporting them with extending their learning is indeed a privilege.

The last I heard Sylvia had progressed onto several other Community Learning courses and – moreover – was reported as one of the most punctual learners in class! Completely worth the perseverance for all involved.

The Project Team

Ros Bauer

Ros Bauer has extensive experience in adult learning and adult language literacy and numeracy (LLN) in Indigenous education contexts. She is committed to adult literacy provision which focuses on developing human capital with sustainable social capital and community capacity building outcomes. Her commitment to this approach is evident in the projects she undertakes such as the work she is currently doing in remote Northern Territory, which led to her award for Excellence in Adult Literacy Numeracy Practice at the 2013 Australian Training Awards. Ros has qualifications in Aboriginal education, TESOL, LLN, Vocational Education and Training; and is principal consultant for her business Ros Bauer Adult Literacy Services.

Michael Chalk

Michael Chalk is an adult educator (language, literacy, numeracy and technology) working in the Adult Community Education (ACE) sector in Victoria, Australia.

He's been involved in state and national digital learning projects such as Access ACE e-Learning Research Circles, and Victorian ACE e-mentor projects, e-learning innovations, e.g. Can You Hear Us? (audio technologies in the classroom), Flexible Learning Leaders and Community Engagement (Australian Flexible Learning Framework).

Keiko Yasukawa

Keiko Yasukawa is a lecturer at the University of Technology Sydney (UTS) in Australia. She has been working at UTS since 1993 in various roles including teaching and coordinating adult education programs, mainly in the area of adult literacy and numeracy. Engagement in the professional field is an important part of Keiko's work. Keiko has held leadership positions in the Australian Council for Adult Literacy and the NSW Adult Literacy and Numeracy Council since 2009.

Keiko's research interest areas are: adult literacy and numeracy policies, pedagogies and practices; critical numeracy and the social studies of mathematics; and precarious employment in Australian higher education. Her recent publications include the edited book with Stephen Black *Beyond economic interests: Critical perspectives on adult literacy and numeracy in a globalised world* (Sense Publishers, 2016). She is the lead editor of *Literacy and Numeracy Studies: an international journal in the education and training of adults.*

Julie Furnivall

Julie Furnivall is a freelance teacher trainer and consultant, with a wide range of skills and expertise developed over forty years in post-compulsory education. Julie has a number of specialisms, but the one that is closest to her heart is English for Speakers of Other Languages. As a trainer, Julie has worked with many hundreds of teachers, tutors, assessors and managers. In addition, she has always taught learners who are improving their skills in literacies. She is proud of the many individuals she has worked with, particularly those who have faced huge barriers in life, yet have still managed to achieve their goals. As well as coaching, teaching and nurturing her learners, Julie has managed numerous projects and initiatives. The most recent was a project about empowering bilingual women who lacked the language skills to be able to communicate confidently about their own health, particularly sexual health.

Tara Furlong

Tara Furlong has twenty years' experience in adult education and training in the private and public sectors in the UK and abroad, specialising in integrated English language, literacies and digital learning. She is involved in delivering professional development via national organisations in the UK, editorial and publication work; and has an established history of designing and implementing systemic curriculum quality initiatives in education providers. She has an ongoing interest in the relationship between multi-modal and contextualised versus abstracted learning; and its mirror in social and literate practice and language across life spheres. As well as work with Designing Futures Ltd, Tara does pro bono work for RaPAL (Research and Practice in Adult Literacies), BALID (British Association for Literacy in Development), is an active local school governor; and is engaged in postgraduate studies in educational leadership with UCL, Institute of Education.

RaPAL (Research and Practice in Adult Literacies)

RaPAL

Research and Practice in Adult Literacies (RaPAL) is the only UK-wide organisation that focuses on the role of literacies in adult life. We promote effective and innovative practices in adult literacies teaching, learning and research; and support adult literacies practitioners and researchers. We enjoy engaging in debates that touch on English language and literacy, numeracy and digital skills across homes, communities and workplaces. Through our members, digital journals, conferences and fora, policy and advocacy work, we are active in Europe and have international links. More information at http://rapal.org.uk/

ACAL (Australian Council for Adult Literacy)

A C A L - Australian Council for Adult Literacy

The Australian Council for Adult Literacy promotes adult literacy and numeracy policy and practice. We provide leadership in Australian debate on adult literacy and numeracy practices and policy. We build understanding of adult literacy and numeracy issues. We advocate on behalf of equitable adult literacy and numeracy provision for all Australians. We build links between people, organisations and systems; the participants and stakeholders in the adult literacy and numeracy field. We work with other organisations on issues of mutual concern. More information at http://acal.edu.au/

Festival of Learning

Festival of Learning Awards showcase and celebrate the wonderful things that learning can achieve for individuals, families, communities and employers. Get involved, and nominate the learners, tutors, projects and employers that deserve recognition, and will inspire others. More information at http://festivaloflearning.org.uk/

"Writing a story for a conference the 'yapa' way i.e. Telling the story of the adult learning centre using traditional art." Left to right: Norissa Nampijinpa Watson, Lavinia Nampijinpa Watson, Gwenneth Napurrurla Nelson and Ros Bauer

Glossary of Acronyms

BTEC Business and Technology Education Council is a provider of vocational qualifications in England, Wales and Northern Ireland

ECDL European Computer Driving Licence qualification

ESL English as a Second Language

ESOL English for Speakers of Other Languages

GCSE General Certificate of Secondary Education in the United Kingdom

NHS National Health Service in the United Kingdom

NVQ National Vocational Qualifications are work based awards in England, Wales and Northern Ireland

OFSTED Office for Standards in Education in the United Kingdom

OCR Oxford Cambridge and Royal Society of the Arts examination board

PTTLS Preparing to Teach in the Lifelong Learning Sector

SVQ Scottish Vocational Qualifications are work based awards in Scotland

TAFE Technical and Further Education in Australia

VCE Victorian Certificate of Education in Victoria, Australia

Index

A

B

C

D

E

F

G

H

I

L

M

N

O

P

R

S

T

V

W